Yerevan Journal

A. Scott Earle

ISBN 978-0-6151-4420-7

Address inquiries to:
Larkspur Books
2440 N. Bogus Basin Road
Boise, ID 83703 USA

larkspur1@cableone.net

First edition

Front cover: Genocide Memorial, Yerevan, Armenia

For Barbara
I missed you. A lot.

Table of Contents

Introduction

After learning, in the early summer of 1993, that I would be going to Armenia, I rummaged through atlases and encyclopedias to learn about the country. I knew only vaguely where Armenia was, and knew nothing about its capital, Yerevan. I discovered a great deal in a short time.

Today's Republic of Armenia is all that remains of a land which had formerly included much of Anatolia (today's eastern Turkey). It is a small country today, a bit smaller than the state of Maryland. It occupies a territory known in the past as "Little Armenia" situated within the southern low (or lesser) Caucasus mountains, on Turkey's eastern border. The Caucasus, one of the earth's more imposing mountain ranges, is divided by a geographic cleft which separates the higher northern mountains from the lower southern range. The high Caucasus rises east of the Black Sea in Russia, and runs diagonally toward the southeast, through Georgia to Azerbaijan on the Caspian sea. It is centered on Mt. Elbrus, a peak that is an impressive 18,506 feet (5,642 meters) high. To the south, the Low Caucasus passes from the eastern end of the Black Sea, into Armenia, Eastern Turkey, western Azerbaijan and thence into Iran. It is low only in comparison, for Mt. Ararat is 17,000 feet (5,185 meters) high.

Many ethnic groups beside the Armenians reside in the Caucasus: Ossetians, Dagestanis, Circassians (Cherkassians,) Abkhazis, Azeris (Azerbaijanis), Chechen, Ingush, Lazis, Kabarda, Adyge and others. Georgia and Armenia are Christian; others—the Circassians, Ingush, Abkhazis, Chechen and Azeris—are Muslim. It's a polyglot region where forty or more languages are spoken. Despite their tribal affinities, the peoples of the Caucasus (including Armenians, but excluding the Azeris) are ethnically quite homogenous.

In the early 19th century, Russia began to expand southward. Armenia became part of the Russian empire in 1828, but the tribes of the Northern Caucasus resisted Russian incursion. Finally, in 1859, they were overcome—sort of—and the entire area became part of Russia. The south ern slope is known today as Trans-Caucasia. By convention, Georgia, Armenia and Azerbaijan, and now Nagorno Karabakh, are the Trans-Caucasian republics.

The Caucasus has always been an unstable region, both seismologically and culturally. The area's ethnically separate groups made trouble for the

USSR as they sought to splinter into independent nationlets. Stalin, never one to fool around, solved the problem temporarily by forcibly relocating these groups eastward to Kazakhstan and Siberia. Many of the expatriates found their way home, however, after World War II, and fighting broke out again in the Caucasus.

The Armenian Republic is the smallest of the former Soviet States, comprising only 0.3% of the USSR's land mass and it is less than two-hundred miles in its longest, north-south, dimension. It has been a stand-alone, independent country only since September of 1990.

Armenia lies below the cleft that divides the High and the Low Caucasus, a feature which some believe should be the boundary between Europe and Asia.* The Arax River flows first south and then east to empty into the Caspian sea. It is a convenient geographic landmark delineating Armenia's western border with Turkey and its southern border with Iran. In reality, Armenia's ethnic and religiously homogenous population marks its borders better than geographic features, especially to the east where there is no natural boundary.

When I visited Armenia in 1993, fifteen new, stand-alone states had recently emerged from the ashes of Soviet disintegration. They had banded loosely together into a Confederation of Independent States (CIS), an entity which included all of the states of the former Soviet Republic. With the breakup of the Soviet Union came chaos. Supply lines broke down. Crime and ethnic turmoil increased. The new states, Armenia more than the others, were burdened with shortages of food, fuel, medical equipment and other necessities.

Almost all Armenians (95%) belong to the the Armenian Orthodox Church, the first of several Christian churches to separate from the early Christian church. The schism occurred in the fourth century and, despite being overrun from time to time, Armenia has remained firmly Christian, whereas the Azeris of Azerbaijan, Armenia's neighbor to the east, are

---

*There is some controversy about the location of Europe's southern intercontinental boundary. This is hardly surprising since Europe and Asia are one land mass and any delineation is artificial. Variously the boundary is considered to be either: (1) the watershed between the Urals and the Caucasus, a line which coincides with the courses of the Don and the Volga rivers; (2) the geographic cleft that separates the High from the Low Caucasus; and (3) the Arax River, the boundary of the former USSR with Turkey and Iran. In 1958, Russian geographers chose the first of these to be the official border, a decision generally accepted today. Armenians prefer the southernmost boundary, however, as this makes Armenia a part of Europe.

Muslim. The two countries have been fighting in the ethnically Armenian enclave of Nagorno Karabakh since the late 1980s (although now, there is an uneasy peace. Azerbaijan lost about 20% of its territory in the conflict.) While in Armenia, I received a lesson in semantics when I asked about the Armenian-Azeri war. I was told—emphatically—that Armenians were *not* fighting a war with Azerbaijan. The Karabakhis are fighting the war; Armenia is only helping.

Because of its location, Armenia is isolated. Azerbaijan lies to the east. Turkey, its arch-enemy, is on the west. Turkey is protective toward Azerbaijan, a country which is ethnically Turkic rather than Caucasian, and which is sitting on an estimated forty billion barrels of off-shore Caspian Sea oil. Turkey has little oil of its own and covets Azerbaijan's. When Armenia intervened in Karabakh, Turkey closed its eastern border and it remains blockaded. While I was in Yerevan,.Georgia, to the north, was embroiled in on-again off-again civil war with its minorities. Further, bandits, presumably Azeris operating in the region, repeatedly blew up the pipeline that carried natural gas from Russia to Armenia. Crossing Armenia's northern border was so dangerous while I was there that US government personnel were forbidden to make the trip between Tbilisi, Georgia's capital, and Yerevan by road.

Iran lies to the south. It is a Muslim nation governed by inflexible Shiites, followers of the fundamentalist doctrines laid down by the late Ayatollah Khomeini. Iran remains, ideologically at least, in the dark ages. Paradoxically, Iran may be Armenia's hope for the future. Despite religous differences, there is an affinity between the countries, historically Persia (Iran) and Armenia were one. [*In 1995 a bridge across the Arax river was completed. Iran and Armenia became trading partners.*]

What follows are notes from a journal kept during a three month stay in Yerevan during the summer and fall of 1993, and on two shorter visits in 1995 and 1996. They are impressions of what was to me a strange land during a time that Armenia, newly emerged from its seventy year union with the USSR, was struggling to become a self-sufficient stand-alone democracy.

In reading what I had written then, now more than a decade later, I came across an occasional candid expression of opinion that seemed in retrospect to be overly explicit, frank or acerbic; these have been modified or omitted where it seemed best to do so. Otherwise, my notes are as I wrote them at the time.

A. Scott Earle
May, 2007

Yerevan Journal

Friday, 23 July 1993

The first rays of the rising sun flooded the cabin of our timeworn Aeroflot T-154 as it began its descent past snow-covered Mt. Ararat. The plane landed a few minutes later and several hundred passengers disembarked onto the concrete runway. A month ago I retired, gave up my plastic surgical practice, and volunteered to come to Armenia. Now, I'm in Yerevan, Armenia's capital, halfway around the world from my home in Idaho. As we moved toward the airport buildings, the U.S. State Department's most recent travel advisory came to mind prompting me to ask the question that travelers have asked for millennia: "What am I doing here?"

"Armenia," the American consular information sheet said, "is a nation undergoing profound political and economic changes. Street demonstrations and other disturbances may occur without warning. In addition, a natural gas and transportation blockade is causing severe food and medical shortages, frequent interruptions in electrical power and shortages of transportation fuel. . . Tourist facilities are not highly developed and many goods and services taken for granted in other countries are not yet available.

"Armed conflict is taking place in and around the Armenian populated area of Nagorno-Karabakh located in Azerbaijan and along the Armenian-Azeri border. Fighting continues on a daily basis, and front lines change frequently. . . There is a severe shortage of basic medical supplies, including disposable needles, anesthetics and antibiotics. Elderly travelers, and those with existing health problems may be at risk due to inadequate medical facilities."

The bit about tourist facilities seemed right on in Paris as I shoved my way toward the Aeroflot counter surrounded by passengers who, like giant ants, carried enormous piles of luggage. Each received a boarding pass, but no seating assignment; seating on Aeroflot planes is catch-as-catch-can. A sign over the counter read: "One bag only may be carried onto the airplane." I had a camera bag and an over-the-shoulder bag with notebook computer, operating loupes (surgical magnifying binoculars), and instruments in it. No way would I check these through.

"Don't worry, no one pays any attention," the French counter attendant said. She was right. Passengers swarmed onto the plane carrying packages and dufflebags that no overhead rack could hold. Young travelers wore rucksacks festooned with sleeping bags, mats and survival gear. "Carry-on" took on new meaning.

The Tupolev 154 is a wide-bodied work-horse plane that seats ten across. It is without first or business-class compartments, but it has plenty of seats for a classless society. Scheduled time of departure was 9:15 p.m. We boarded on time and and then waited for three hours while the cabin air was replaced with cigarette smoke. There were no "Fasten Seat Belt" and no "No Smoking" signs. Passengers, all furiously smoking, stood in the aisles during takeoff, displaying a fatalistic philosophy; "if the plane crashes, what difference does it make?" The plane was old and filthy. Carpets, originally maroon, were black with grime. The seats might have come from an abandoned long-ago cinema; many were broken. A pervasive odor of urine wafted through the aisles from the plane's toilets.

Despite the plane's slovenly condition, the trip was smooth from takeoff to landing five hours later in Yerevan. Once airborne, passengers turned down seat backs to form tables for their bottles of vodka. The drinkers were noisy at first, but soon they slept quietly, and the rush of the engines was the only sound. Three young soldiers had walked onto the plane on crutches and were now sleeping side-by-side in bulkhead seats. They had been wounded in Nagorno Karabakh, the mountainous Armenian enclave within Azerbaijan, coming home after treatment abroad. Passengers had piled the bulkhead full of baggage to support their injured legs.

I didn't care much for the flight. In the event, there was nothing to do but to lie back and put in the time. The Armenian General Benevolent Union, an organization known to every Armenian in the world as "the AGBU," sponsored my trip. Their representative in New Jersey had reassured me. Armenian pilots, she told me, are excellent. I believed her, but what about their tired old airplanes? I thought of Meteora in northern Greece where ancient monasteries are situated atop sheer rock spires. Dangling from ropes, woven baskets carry monks and supplies to the top. When asked how they know when to change the rope, the monks invariably reply, "When it breaks, of course..." I hope not to be on an Aeroflot plane when the rope breaks.*

---

* Aeroflot did not have a great safety record. A Tupolev 154 went down in January 1994, in Siberia, killing one hundred and twenty people. The following March an Airbus A-310, en route from Moscow to Hong Kong, flew into a

Our plane roared uneventfully through the night and shortly after dawn touched down to a smooth landing. We deplaned and walked across the runway into an unlighted room in the airport. A lone official sat in a little confessional, slowly, slowly, processing passports. Pressed together, travelers sweltered and fanned themselves with opened passports. Eventually I passed through and emerged into a milling throng waiting for relatives and friends to appear. A group of four stood beyond the crowd. One man, taller than the others, held up a sign with my name on it. I recognized Dr. Gagik Stamboltsian, Chief of the Yerevan Plastic and Reconstructive Surgical Center, from a photo that the AGBU had provided. He is a tall man who looks more European than Armenian. (I learned later that his family came to Yerevan from Istanbul, as his name, Stamboltsian, suggests.)

The other three included an attractive black-haired woman, Dr. Armine Kharatian, the Center's Chief of Anesthesia (her name is pronounced Armi-NEH; the last syllable of Armenian words is usually accented), and a second surgeon, Dr. Garegin Babloyan. The fourth person was Mike McIntyre, an American and the Center's Administrative Director. After introductions, Mike said that it would take two hours or more to unload the plane. He would wait and pick up my luggage, filled with the medical supplies that had been donated by several hospitals. I understood now why passengers carried on so much luggage—they wanted to avoid waiting at the airport.

We left Mike and drove into the city. Long lines of trucks are parked along the roads leading to the airport. Azerbaijan and its Muslim allies are blockading Armenia and the waiting trucks show how important air transport is for the country. Because there is a fuel shortage, there is almost no traffic on the road. We pass through hilly brown countryside. Flocks of goats graze along the road, and the hills are covered with trellised vines.

Yerevan is a green city with tree-filled open areas, interspersed with clusters of ponderous stone buildings. An enormous bronze statue of a woman holding a partly sheathed sword stands on a hilltop overlooking the city. "Mother Armenia," the doctors tell me. The apartment house

---

mountainside in Siberia. The pilot's fifteen year old son was at the controls when it crashed. Seventy five passengers died. In April, 1994, the Airline Passengers Association recommended against flying on Aeroflot, citing shoddy maintenance procedures, gross overloading, and lack of safety standards. Unfortunately, there was no other way to reach parts of interior Russia, former Soviet states, and various contiguous countries.

where I'll be living for the next three months looks abandoned and dirty, its entry unswept and trash-filled. A decrepit, inoperative elevator hangs askew at the bottom of an open shaft. Its unevenly welded framework might have been constructed by a child using an adult erector set.

The doctors carried my luggage upstairs. The stair risers are crumbling and reinforcing rods show through on the landings. Light reaches the stairwell through broken. grimy windows. I feel like an extra in *Escape from New York*, caught in a post-cataclysmic city. Surprisingly, the apartment is not bad. The furniture is old, but it will serve. Patterned oriental rugs cover the floors. There is a black and white TV, although there are only two channels and reception is poor. The kitchen is equipped with a microwave and a Japanese refrigerator. The bathroom has a cast-iron tub and directly over it hangs an enormous clear plastic water tank with an electrical heating element. It is the only source of hot water in the apartment.

I cleaned up and climbed a flight to Armine Kharatian's apartment. It is attractively furnished, a surprise, considering the building's outside appearance. A meal was waiting. Aram, Armine's husband, a man in his late thirties, arrived on crutches and took his seat at the head of the table. He is a geologist, but has multiple sclerosis and has not been able to work for several years. Armine introduced me to her mother-in-law, Ala, a pleasant blonde Ukrainian lady. Their dark-haired, twelve year old daughter is another Ala. The Alas served fresh green beans in a cheese sauce, roast chicken, sliced tomatoes, cucumbers, and hard cheese.

The lunch was agreeable, the more so as both Armine and Gagik speak English. Armine's is excellent; Gagik just gets by. Bottles of vodka and cognac were on the table. As Gagik offered a toast, Mike McIntyre arrived carrying the enormous suitcase that I bought in a thrift shop in the States. It is crammed full of sutures, lidocaine, disposable needles and syringes, surgical sponges, dressing materials, and other supplies that the Unit does not have.

After Mike ate, we drove to the hospital. Yerevan is decaying: fading paint, shabby buildings, rusty fixtures, and pot-holes. Beneath the dilapidation, however, I sense a gracious city with wide streets and many parks. Few cars are on the road; most are older Fiat clones, although I saw several new American and Japanese sports utility vehicles. Mike dismissed them as "Mafia status symbols."

"No relation to the real Mafia," he said. "These are Armenians, but they function the same way and that's what they're called."

The AGBUs Plastic and Reconstructive Center, "the Unit," is located in the Mikaelian Surgical Institute, a large, six-story building, located on the heights above the city. The building is faced with an orange stone. Most Yerevan buildings are built of brownish-pink stone, a form of compressed volcanic ash ("tufa"), that the Armenians call "toof." Yerevan has long been known as "the Rose City" from the brownish pink color of the stone.

The Plastic and Reconstructive Surgical Center ("PRSC") occupies the fourth floor of a hospital wing. Ten clean, well furnished rooms each with two beds, open off a corridor covered with what may be the world's longest oriental carpet. The beds are all occupied.

We made rounds. I was impressed with how the surgeons have treated war injuries from Nagorno Karabakh. Their results seem to compare favorably with our own in the United States. True, we see few war wounds in the States, but we have similar patients injured in motor vehicle accidents, motorcycles, especially, and in the senseless violence of the inner city.

Several patients were admitted for minor surgery. I was surprised to learn that outpatient surgery is almost never carried out. Patients are admitted for simple procedures such as correction of protuberant ears, or removal of small skin lesions, and then remain in the hospital for many days. The surgeons explain that they are under pressure to keep the unit's beds full. As Gagik Stamboltsian explained this, I thought of my own resident rotations through inefficient Veterans Administration Hospitals where we were continually reminded that we must keep the bed census high. As a consequence, patients remained in VA hospitals long after their recovery.*

We continued our tour. The operating suite is equipped with two new sterilizers, modern anesthesia machines, gleaming OR lights, patient monitors, and other up-to-date American equipment. Similarly, the intensive care unit, located for some unknown reason far away from the OR, is beautifully equipped. It has four intensive care and four post-surgical recovery beds. Each bed has piped-in oxygen, suction, individual lighting, and full monitoring equipment, all in accordance with American hospital standards. Impressive, but why is the ICU located at the farthest end

---

* I once ran afoul of the system by refusing to admit a healthy veteran who wanted a warm bed for the winter. He complained to his senator. The senator wrote a no-nonsense letter to the hospital: "admit this man." I regret that I trashed the letter, for it was written by John F. Kennedy, then the junior senator from Massachusetts.

of the hospital? And a big question: what type and what volume of plastic surgery justifies such a lavish setup? Clearly the AGBU spent tons of money to construct this center.

I learned about the PRSC from an article in the *Plastic Surgical News*, a trade newsletter. It described a plastic surgical unit that had just opened in Yerevan, the only facility of its kind in Armenia. An earthquake that ravaged the northern part of the country in December of 1988 led to the Center's construction. Armenians in America and elsewhere contributed heavily to the AGBU's earthquake relief efforts. The chief of the plastic surgical program at Yale came to Armenia on an early relief flight. He saw that reconstructive surgical services were needed, but in Armenia plastic surgery was not even recognized as a surgical specialty. Some earthquake victims were sent to the States for care; an impractical solution given the number of casualties. Local care was needed.

The AGBU took on the project. One only has to visit the Unit to recognize what an enormous amount of work, organization, and money was expended. A physical plant was necessary. Personnel—surgeons, anesthesiologists and nurses—had to be trained. The United States Agency for International Development (AID) pitched in to provide 1.4 million dollars, a sum that the AGBU matched. There was now plenty of money, enough to build the Center in the existing Mikaelian Surgical Institute, and to arrange for a cadre of doctors and nurses to go to the States for training.

The article in the *Plastic Surgery News*, and later conversations with AGBU personnel suggested that the Unit had some startup problems. The organization wanted a senior plastic surgeon to go to Armenia for six months to operate, teach, identify problems, and suggest solutions. In short, the organization wanted a hired gun. ("Hired" was figurative; only room, board and transportation were offered.)

I had recently retired as the Director of Plastic Surgery in a large teaching hospital and become an emeritus professor in the associated medical school. At loose ends, I was casting around for a project in which my knowledge and experience would matter. Given my background, I would be able both to teach, and to evaluate how the Unit functioned. Six months was too long, however. The past winter in Yerevan had been bitterly cold. There had been no fuel or electricity for heating. Fifty years earlier, I had experienced winter while serving in the US Army's 10th Mountain Division. I'm too old now to play cold weather survival games. Three months might be too long, too, but at least it should be endurable. I signed on.

Monday, 26 July 1993

I walked downtown yesterday with Armine Kharatian and her daughter Ala. I saw almost no English, except for an occasional trilingual street sign in Armenian, Russian and English. We visited a large underground department store where few goods were displayed other than a selection of shoes, imported from China. Other shops are located in the basements of buildings. Their shelves were empty, or sparsely supplied at best. We walked past several flower markets. Flowers are plentiful, and many people were buying. The rest of the weekend was devoted to unpacking, cleaning, and organizing the apartment. Its owners have fled to Bulgaria to escape the hard times. The apartment is filled with their sheet-covered belongings.

Armine was at my door at 8:00 o'clock this morning. The Unit's contract driver, Abo, was waiting in his van with Mike McIntyre, Marianne Hess, an American ICU nurse who has been here for almost a year, and two Armenian secretaries. Both are named Nune (Nu-NEH, a common Armenian girls' name.) One is "tall Nune," the other "short Nune." Mike has also been here for a year and he seems both wise and knowledgeable. He and Marianne will help me define problems and personalities. We chatted in the van, and later in the hospital over small cups of silty, boiled Armenian coffee. Mike stressed that it will be important for me to identify trouble areas. It will be equally important to recognize that here, more than in most places, problems may have no solution.

First, Mike said, there is the Mikaelian Surgical Institute's Director. The AGBU personnel in the States had previously warned me about him. Dr. Hamlet Tamasian is difficult, they said. I mentioned this to Mike. He smiled. Whatever I had been told, he said, had been understated; the Director is unpredictable, ruthless and certifiably crazy. We didn't have time to talk further, for Gagik came in to tell me that patients were waiting to be seen. We walked to his office through a cluster of patients and relatives. Half a dozen children had cleft lip deformities. All had been operated on before. The original repairs consisted simply of surgically paring the margins of the gaping defects in their lips, and then pulling the raw edges together with heavy sutures. The children's lips are scarred, tight, asymmetric, and have no semblance of normal contour. We may be able to improve the contour but I don't know how we can eradicate the wide, irregular scars.

The other Armenian surgeon, Dr. Garegin Babloyan, introduced the little patients and their parents to me. He is a slight, serious, ingratiating man of about thirty who speaks English well. Mike tells me that he is devious and a dedicated Russophile. Garegin evidently has a special interest in cleft lip surgery and has read everything on the subject in the Unit's library. He has a bilateral cleft lip scheduled and has found twelve different ways to correct the condition. He is agonizing about which method to use. I told him that an academic approach is healthy so long as one maintains perspective, noting also that whenever many methods are recommended, it usually indicates that there is no one good method.

The two surgeons, Gagik Stamboltsian and Garegin Babloyan, are quite different. Gagik is tall and brusque, Garegin is slight and earnest. Gagik's English is poor, yet he manages to get his ideas across. Garegin's English is good, but he is obsequious. Because of their disparate interests I would think that they would complement each other. Later, when I met again with Mike, I asked him about Gagik and Garegin. Another problem, he said. There is serious friction between the two surgeons and between Garegin and the rest of the medical staff. In a unit staffed with few people, interpersonal conflict means trouble.

Two of this morning's patients had the sequelae of electrical burns. One, a boy of nine, lost both his left arm at the shoulder joint and his penis flush with his abdomen. The scar on his shoulder is tightly adherent to the underlying shoulder blade and in danger of ulcerating. The boy and his father are not interested in doing anything about this; they want the boy to have a new penis. His external urethral opening seems adequate, so there is no need for immediate surgery and it would be better to postpone reconstructive surgery until he is older. Possibly the AGBU could send him to the States for this. Alternatively, a surgeon experienced in penile reconstruction might come to Armenia when the child has reached an appropriate age. Father and son departed, clearly disappointed with my advice.

The other patient, a man of thirty-five, has a gaping hole involving the lower half of his right forearm where four inches of bone are exposed. Large tissue defects, such as this one, especially when bone is exposed, are best treated by covering them with a microsurgical free tissue transfer, a "free flap," using tissue surgically separated from a part of the body from which it can be spared. Microsurgical techniques are used to approximate blood vessels and restore circulation to the transferred tissue. Free flaps have many advantages, but they also require an experienced team of surgeons, and specialized equipment. The Unit has an excellent operating microscope, microsurgical instruments and sutures, and we have the experience. We scheduled the man for the procedure.

When all of the patients had been seen, Gagik and I visited the hospital's orthopaedic unit where many of the patients are casualties from Nagorno Karabakh. We had been asked to see a five-year old child with a large, open, through-and-through gunshot wound of her foot, with exposed bone and tendons. Her wounds might close spontaneously by scarring if we wait six months or so, but it would be better to close the wounds now, so we added her to our schedule.

Mike, Gagik and I talked more about the Armenian hospital system during lunch break. Repair of a split earlobe is the only case scheduled for tomorrow. The patient has been waiting in the hospital for days, and will remain for three days or longer after her surgery. Split lobes come from wearing earrings that are too heavy, or from having one (or both) pulled off in a fight (common in motorcycle gang women), or even by a baby grabbing a shiny earbob. The surgery is a simple half hour procedure performed under local anesthesia in a doctor's office or outpatient clinic. Not so, here, Mike said. We do things the Soviet way. It will be an uphill fight to change the system.

The entire English-speaking staff, except for Garegin, have now warned me about the Director. At least I don't have to worry about him for a while, for he is in the United States. The AGBU's medical coordinator told me, during one of many phone conversations, that Dr. Tamasian would be visiting the organization's office in New Jersey. She added that he is reputed to be an excellent surgeon. He also had been a medical school classmate of the Armenian Minister of Health.

"You know," the Coordinator said, "the Director used to be a pleasant person. Then he became dictatorial, unpredictable, overreactive, and nasty."

"In any event," she said, "don't worry, I'll take care of him. He's coming to America. He'll be on my territory. We'll come to an understanding and I'll fix things up. His wife is an obstetrician and gynecologist and she's here now, a lovely woman. Their two children are in school in the States. I spent four hours with her yesterday, and had lunch with her today. Her husband is coming in a few days. I'll set him straight then."

I told Gagik how she planned to reshape the Director during his stay in America, and how he would return to Armenia a new person.

"I have told her about him." Gagik said, shaking his head. "He is crazy. She not listen. He won't change. I work with him. I know him."

Gagik had warned me that there would be many patients with burn injuries, and this afternoon several more showed up. All need surgery. Burn scars contract as they heal so burn patients often develop joint contractures. It is then necessary to divide, or remove the scar, and fill the resulting gap appropriately, usually with skin grafts in order to restore joint motion. We scheduled their surgery, as we had for those we saw this morning. Why, I asked Gagik are there were so many burn patients?

"Because of terrible winter," he answered. "People do crazy things, use petrol for fires, other bad things and then get burned."

The AGBU's news-magazine ran pictures of people in Yerevan standing in the last winter's deep snow, cutting down trees for fuel. It is little wonder that so many Armenians have departed for Bulgaria, Belarus, even the United States, wherever there are relatives who will take them in.

Marianne wanted to visit shops on the way home and asked if there was anything I wanted. I listed paper towels, ketchup, liquid soap for the kitchen, and something to put on the tough Armenian bread that one or the other of the Alas brings down each evening. I suspected that there would be little chance of finding any of the things that I mentioned. To our surprise, we found jars of apricot jam in one of the stores, made here in Armenia. Free enterprise is on the way.

"When you see something that you want, or think that you may want, get it now," she told me, "because it won't be there tomorrow."

We bought jam and Snickers bars. Strangely, candy, cigarettes, liquor, beer, and other non-essential luxuries arrive from Europe, Canada and the United States. They are popular, although expensive, items that are sold in little street stands and kiosks. Armine says that these have appeared since the Soviet breakup. She doesn't like them. They sell only luxury goods and prey on common people rather than serving them, she says. When Armenia was part of the USSR, there were only government stores. They were well supplied, then, but no longer. Street businesses, shops and kiosks seem to be taking their place.

After Abo dropped me off, I called home. Wife Barbara had planned to join me in Armenia. I told her that it would be best not to make the long and unpleasant trip. These days Yerevan is not a good place to visit. Maybe later.

I see decay and shoddiness everywhere. The former reflects the bad times, the latter is a reflection of Soviet ethos. Nothing is screwed on straight, nothing is flush. Construction is never quite completed. Plumbing is poorly installed. Pipes are crooked and leak. Drain systems are left with open joints. Windows are cracked and masonry crumbles. Holes are everywhere. Anything that can rust is rusted. Enormous potholes turn the streets into obstacle courses. Here, it seems that if it's broken, don't fix it. I'm in a different world on another planet. This evening, I went up to Armine's apartment to get newspapers. Even newspapers, the ultimate expendable item, are saved. Armine uses them for what I want them for;

to line trash buckets. Strange, how many uses there are for commonplace commodities, and how they take on uncommon value when no longer available. Plastic bags, the flimsy ones that supermarkets in the States use, are treasures here. I use them to bring my lunch to the hospital. If I turn my back, the bag disappears.

Tuesday, 27 July 1993

Even though Monday is the designated "clinic day" for new patients, they arrive whenever they can find transportation. This morning we saw a child with a partial ear amputation, an attractive fifteen year old girl with a poorly repaired cleft lip, and a twelve year old boy with a cleft lip and palate. The boy's palate has been repaired three times and is still wide open. He has a misshapen upper jaw, his lip is short, tight and scarred. His speech, typical of patients with open clefts of the palate, is terrible. I don't need to understand Armenian to recognize hyper-resonance and poor articulation. I hardly know what to recommend for this child. In the States he would be evaluated and cared for by a specialist cleft palate team. He should have orthognathic (jaw straightening) surgery with bone grafting to correct his malocclusion, and prosthodontia to fill in the wide cleft with an appropriate prosthetic dental device None of these services are available here. For now, I suggested only a cross-lip flap to improve his appearance. (A "cross-lip flap" is a wedge of lip tissue borrowed from the lower lip and used to replace tissue missing at the site of the original cleft. The procedure may dramatically improve the appearance of patients who lack substance in the upper lip.)

Garegin had already talked to the child's parents about the operation. Gagik says that he can't see it. I don't know whether he *really* can't see it, for the procedure is clearly indicated, or he can't see it because of hostility toward Garegin. I'm trying to figure out the the two surgeon's relationship. Both surgeons had specialty training in Russia; Gagik in microsurgery and Garegin in vascular surgery. Both worked in the Mikaelian Surgical Institute. They were chosen, long distance and sight unseen, from a list of young Armenian surgeons who were interested in going to America for specialty training in plastic surgery. In addition, two anesthesiologists, Armine Kharatian and Karen Manvelyan (Karen is a man's name in Armenia) whom I have not yet met, and six nurses were chosen. The ten Armenians spent a year at Yale University Hospital with all expenses paid by the AGBU, although the organization would not pay for their families to come with them. The trainees returned last winter; the Unit opened then.

Another surgeon, Leon Torossian, has since joined the staff. He is young, unmarried, and has an eye for the ladies, especially for tall Nune, the willowy senior secretary. Leon is enthusiastic, intelligent, thorough, and has a good command of English. He also gets along well with everyone. He has had microsurgical training and worked with Gagik before Gagik went to the States. Leon was able to spend three months in Austria on a plastic surgical service, so at least he knows what the specialty is about.

Microsurgery is a separate specialty only in the the former Soviet Republic and in China. Elsewhere it is considered to be a surgical technique based on miniaturization of standard surgical methodology, one that is used by many surgical specialties for reconstructive procedures. I was surprised to learn that there was a separate microsurgical service here at the Mikaelian Institute. I asked Gagik whether the service performed many operations. "Yes," he said, "casualties go directly there from Karabakh."

Strange. Who decides whether a patient requires a microsurgical reconstructive procedure, versus a simpler one such as a local flap, a skin graft, tissue expansion, or whatever?*

Today Leon showed me a soldier with multiple shrapnel wounds and a Volkmann's contracture involving his right forearm.† Leon operated on the man three months ago. He freed the scarred median nerve and tried

---

* A 'flap' is a tongue of skin and subcutaneous tissue used to close an adjacent defect. A flap remains attached to the body and its blood supply is not interrupted. A "free flap," described earlier, is transiently separated from its blood supply, but the principle is similar. "Musculocutaneous" and "fasciocutaneous" flaps include overlying skin and underlying vascularized muscle, or "fascia," a tough tissue layer.
A "graft" is tissue, most commonly skin, but sometimes other tissues, that has been separated completely from the body and transplanted to a distant area. A graft gains a new blood supply over a period of time.
"Tissue expansion" is a method of slowly stretching skin and underlying tissue, using a plastic bag filled gradually with saline solution. Once expanded, the stretched tissue can be used to cover adjacent defects.

†Volkmann's ischemic contracture is named eponymously for Richard von Volkmann (1830-1889), a prominent German surgeon who described it in 1889. In this condition, injured muscle, tightly confined within an anatomic compartment, swells so much that its circulation is cut off—it becomes "ischemic." If the muscle is not promptly decompressed it undergoes "necrosis" or death, and is slowly replaced with scar tissue. When this occurs in an extremity, it is followed by withering and loss of function.

to reestablish circulation using vein grafts. It was more surgery than he should have attempted without help, as he now recognizes. Today, I find that the man has loss of median nerve function in his hand, a pulseless forearm and wrist, and fixed contractures of wrist and hand. I don't know any extremity condition that is harder to treat. Still, I think we should explore the arm, do a nerve graft to try to provide some sensation to the hand, and lengthen the contracted flexor muscles and tendons.

After we finished seeing patients, I rode with Abo who was driving Mike McIntyre to the International Red Cross Hospital, a rehabilitation facility on the outskirts of Yerevan. Mike's wife, Sue, a physical therapist, works there. It was an opportunity for me to see the city. Pollution is terrible. Mount Ararat lies thirty miles southwest of Yerevan and serves as a gauge of air quality. When the pollution is bad, as it is today, the mountain is invisible, obscured by a gray-brown haze. When the air is clear, as it is occasionally, Ararat dominates the horizon. It is a huge mountain and even now, in late July, the upper half is snow covered. I'd love to go there, but Armenia's border with Turkey is closed. I wonder whether it would be possible to drive from Athens through Turkey to Armenia? [*After returning to the States, I found that a State Department advisory strongly advises against driving in eastern Turkey and notes further that climbing Mt. Ararat is particularly dangerous. The danger is from the PKK, the Kurdish terrorist organization. Some believe that both the Armenians and the Greeks are assisting the PKK. If so, it is not surprising in view of Turkey's past and present relationships with these countries.*]

Mike had Abo pull over as we came abreast of a housing development. He pointed to a complex of ten apartment buildings. Each building is thirteen stories high. Eight are complete and occupied. Four giant construction cranes loom above the two that are unfinished.

"Look at those buildings," Mike said, "and tell me how you'd like to be in one if an earthquake struck?"

His question has frightening implications. The walls in the unfinished buildings are not in place in the upper levels and the buildings' skeletons are exposed. There is a heavy central column—a vertical axis—with enormous octagonal concrete plates one floor apart, shish-kabobed on it. The plates serve as bases for each floor, and as a ceiling for the floor below. Smaller vertical supports at each of the eight outer angles give a neat polygonal configuration. The eight outside walls are then filled in with concrete building blocks. I know little about architecture or construction, but these high buildings don't look as if they would take a whole lot of shaking. Mike muttered something about "house of cards." And if the concrete is as shoddy as that in our apartment house, a strong earthquake, epicenter Yerevan, will give graphic meaning to the term "civil disaster."

Mike then posed a second question:

"Can you believe that those buildings looked exactly like that three years ago when the Soviet Union broke up?" [*December 21, 1991, is the formal date for the dissolution of the USSR.*]

I didn't understand what he meant. Then I realized why there are so many unfinished buildings and rusty construction cranes throughout Yerevan.

"They were all caught in the same time warp," he explained. "When the Soviet Union fell apart, all construction in Armenia—and everywhere else in the Soviet Union, I imagine—stopped. The workers weren't paid, so they walked away. Construction in Armenia has not advanced by a single brick since then. The cranes and the unfinished buildings have been in a time capsule, on hold for three years."

Being in Armenia has made me aware of the historical enormity of the Soviet Union's dissolution. In the future, I suspect, the break-up of the USSR will be viewed as one of history's great social cataclysms.

Wednesday, 28 July 1993

Armenia is a country of contrasts. The produce sold in street markets is plentiful and excellent, but there is almost no fuel. The fruit and vegetables are the best I have ever eaten anywhere. Tomatoes are sweet, juicy, red, and thin-skinned. Yet petrol stations are all closed, and the only fuel available comes from tank trucks spotted along the roadways. Cars surround them, like satellites, as drivers wait to get twenty-liter jerricans filled, one for the car, one for the trunk. When I ask where the gas comes from, nobody seems to know. I get different answers—from Georgia, or from Russia. For all I know, the trucks may go north and then swing down into Azerbaijan and buy petrol there. Fuel is about the only commodity that arrives in Armenia by land, brought in by fuel trucks running in convoys for mutual safety.

So much has changed here. Before the Soviet Union fell apart, everything hummed along under Mother Russia. My 1968 *Encyclopedia Britannica* noted that Yerevan was one of the most important manufacturing centers in the Soviet Union. Metal and rubber goods, tires, computers, and chemicals were manufactured here. Aluminum was produced here, using electricity generated by hydroelectric stations on the Razdan River and by the Caucasus's only nuclear reactor. [*The reactor, considered a hazard, was shut down in 1989, a few months after the earthquake; it has since reopened.*)]. Now the factories are at a standstill.

The Razdan River arises from Lake Sevan, one of the world's largest mountain lakes. The river drops the better part of a mile of elevation before running through a deep gorge in the center of Yerevan to join the Arax river a few miles to the west. Armenia now has a severe shortage of electrical power. I asked the doctors if the hydroelectric plants still function, but nobody seems to know. If they are functioning, they are not producing nearly enough power for the country's needs.

Before the breakup, roads were well maintained, and the state supported ambitious public works. Yerevan has a modern, 80,000 capacity sports stadium built on the heights above the Razdan. The Armenians tell me that their soccer teams are excellent. An ultramodern Youth Center stands on the hillside across from my apartment, a landmark that can be seen from everywhere in the city. It has a massive, fortress-like, stone foundation dotted with soaring arched windows. Above, there are seven levels of terraces; these in turn are topped by a fifteen-story circular hotel with a restaurant and viewing floor on the top level. The total effect is that of an extra-galactic Disney World castle. The Youth Center has fallen on hard times. Now it is known simply as "The Motel" and functions as an apartment complex. From close by I see that it is run down, and surrounded by crudely built ghetto-like houses where packs of dogs and children run in the streets.

It is the same with many other public works (I use the term "public works" as a convenience; everything is public here). Projects may be striking when seen from afar, but on closer view they are either unfinished, or falling into decrepitude with falling cornices, peeling paint, and general disrepair.

Yerevan also has many monuments; statues are dotted throughout the city. They, at least, are holding up well. Some, of various notables—all are men—are so striking that I wish I knew more about the personages represented. Armine tells me who they are as we walk. Writers (Khatchatur Abovian, Mikael Nalbandian, Ovanes Tumanian), revolutionaries (Stepan Shahumian), an architect (Alexander Tamanian), statesmen (Alexander Griboyedov), composers (Alexander Spendiarov), poets (Avetik Isaakian, David Sasunsky, Sayat-Nova) and politicians (Gukas Gukasian) are honored by statuary. They are only names to me, unknown in the West. When I said as much to Armine, she answered that the West *should* know about them.

Whenever I walk on Yerevan' streets, I am aware that I am a foreigner. Occasionally people ask in broken English whether I am American, or English, or German. Westerners tend to be tall; at six feet two inches, I feel like the tallest person in Armenia. Westerners are usually well dressed, even in casual clothes. We are pink-skinned and we look alien. It will ever be so, for most Armenians look like Armenians; they are shorter, their skin is darker. They have curly black hair. The men usually need a shave. The Armenian nose, big, beaked, with a dropped tip, is almost universal.

I thought that their nose was an ethnic characteristic that Armenians would wear with pride. Not so; many want nose jobs. Yesterday, two young women, relatives of doctors in the hospital, came to the Unit. They wanted rhinoplasties. Both were good candidates for the operation. I was taken unaware, but common sense should have forewarned me. Armine told me several days ago that if anyone started doing noses in Armenia there would be no end to it. (Armine, an attractive lady, had her rhinoplasty done while she was in New Haven.) I'm not happy; I didn't come here to do cosmetic surgery. This is something I have to think about.

Later in the afternoon, another young woman, a hospital employee, appeared. She, too, wants a rhinoplasty. It doesn't take a mathematician to see that we have here the potential for an Armenian pyramid game. Do one, get three, do three get nine, and soon we're up to our noses in noses. Clearly, we either go into the rhinoplasty business or we don't. A compromise is not going to work.

After thinking about it, I said, "No nose jobs." It may be my puritan upbringing, but it doesn't seem appropriate for visiting surgeons to use donated facilities and operating time to provide three-thousand dollar cosmetic operations for free.

Later, I talked with Mike about rhinoplasties.

"You're right, of course," he said; "but wait until the crazy Director gets back. He'll pressure you to do them on his Mafia friends and then on friends of his friends. You can't know how deeply entrenched the Armenian Mafia is. Favors drive the system and he's part of it, or he wouldn't be where he is. Worse, he's crazy. Everyone knows that he's crazy. The Minister of Health knows it, the President knows it, but he has connections...."

I helped Gagik release a burn scar of an upper eyelid. We used a full thickness skin graft from behind the ear to cover the large defect of the upper lid. It only went so-so. Gagik hadn't taken a post-auricular graft before and it came out fragmented, so I had to take another. After that, we explored the radial nerve in a soldier who was shot in the arm a few months ago. I would have waited, as he is showing signs of spontaneous recovery, but it was not unreasonable to look. We found localized scar reaction, and Gagik freed the nerve up at that point. The amount of scarring was not impressive, however, and I suspect that we didn't help the patient all that much. Gagik is an impatient surgeon. He operates using a rending technique, bluntly pulling tissues apart as he goes. A lot of surgeons, including some very effective ones, operate this way, but I think it less harmful to use sharp dissection to separate tissue planes.

Thursday, 29 July 1993

This morning I helped Gagik with an abdominoplasty ("tummy-tuck") on an obese woman. It was the first one that he has done. I'm beginning to wonder how much hands-on surgery he and Garegin did in the States, and how much of their experience was observational. The latter may be valuable for fully trained surgeons, but surgeons-in-training need to operate. Surgical training programs vary greatly. Some have a large volume of surgery for trainees, others do not. When there is not enough to go around, surgical fellows—a category into which I suspect the Armenians fell—end up observing and not operating.

We have a visitor. Dr. Wan Ho, a plastic surgeon with a primary interest in surgery of the hand, arrived yesterday. He is on the staff of a large Kaiser Permanente Hospital near Los Angeles. He brought instruments and small joint prostheses with him, planning to reconstruct arthritic hands. Gagik either didn't know this, or he couldn't find any patients who needed the surgery. On balance, this is probably OK. The Surgical Institute's postoperative therapeutic services, necessary after such surgery, are nonexistent, so I question how useful Dr. Ho's joint replacement surgery would be other than to demonstrate the operation. No matter, there's plenty of hand surgery to do and he'll be busy for the two weeks that he'll be here.

Friday, 30 July 1993

Today I did secondary cleft lips revisions on two girls, one nine and the other fifteen years old. Both were difficult because the original surgery was so crude. I was pleased with our results, but the patients and their parents may be disappointed. Even though surgeons explain beforehand that results can never be perfect, people hear what they want to hear. Some expect perfection, and no amount of pre-operative explanation will disabuse them of this expectation. Then, inevitably, they are disappointed by anything less.

Saturday, 31 July 1993

I called Barbara this morning and got through to wish her "Happy Birthday" and to tell her how much I miss her. She told me home news and had many questions: "What do you eat?";"What do you do in the evening?"; "What do you do on weekends?"; "Who do you talk to?" I described my routine, and told her that loneliness is the biggest problem, especially on weekends. We are not doing enough surgery for me to feel challenged, and there is little to keep me occupied when I'm not in the hospital. While English is the second language in many countries, Russian is the second language here—a language as incomprehensible for me as Armenian is—so there is little chance to talk with others. I explore the city, read, enter journal notes into my notebook computer, and listen to my little Sony shortwave radio.

An AGBU flight arrives tomorrow. Five large boxes that I sent ahead to New Jersey should be on the plane. They contain personal items: batteries, books, food, audio tapes, etc., as well as supplies that we need in the OR: instruments, plastic surgical sutures (we have none), lidocaine (we're out of that, too), etc. With two American surgeons here, we should get as much done as we can, but we do need supplies.

This morning Armine, little Ala, and I, met Marianne and Wan Ho. We walked to the Matenadaran (the word means "repository" in old Armenian) a beautiful library built in 1957 for the purpose of housing ancient manuscripts. The Matenadaran is a Yerevan landmark. It contains one of the world's largest collections of manuscripts including some fragments from the sixth century A.D., and there are complete books from the eighth century on. All are written on vellum and many are exquisitely illuminated. Most are bibles and religious works, but some are translations from much older Greek manuscripts that are known today only in Armenian translations.

The institute is dedicated to St. Mesrop Mashdots (or Mashtots, ca. 350-439 A.D.). Mashdots was a priest and scholar. He is credited with "inventing" the Armenian alphabet in the fifth century. The original alphabet, as he devised it—working, presumably, with a pre-existing base—remains in use today. It has little resemblance to other alphabets. Many of the characters resemble "U" s with little hooks protruding here and there. Armenians say that it is a good alphabet; each of its 39 letters accurately represents a sound in their language. The Armenian language is also unique. Although basically Indo-European, much of its vocabulary comes from Persian loan words (Armenia and Persia were one country at various times in the past). Xenophon, the Greek general and historian who led the retreat of his defeated mercenaries out of Persia and across Anatolia to the Black Sea in 401 B.C., wrote in his *Anabasis* that the inhabitants of Armenian villages that he passed through understood his Persian interpreters.

The Matenadaran is a handsome contemporary building that shows much of the formal busy-ness and detail that characterize Armenian art. A large stone statue of St. Mesrop, seated before a tablet showing the Armenian alphabet, graces the approach, and tall statues of Armenian philosophers and literary personages stand in a row along the front of the building. Sculpture and architecture have always been the strongest of the Armenian arts, and the Matenadaran carries on that tradition.

Manuscripts are displayed in a circular room on the building's second floor. These show the use of illumination and calligraphy over the centuries. The rest of the library is used for preservation, restoration, and study of books and manuscripts. Since being moved to Yerevan from Echmiadzin, the seat of the Armenian church a few miles outside the city, the collection has doubled in size through donations from around the world and coalescence with other collections.

Armine translated as a curator showed us around and told us about the museum, its manuscripts and their illuminations. These are striking and rival those of religious miniaturists active elsewhere during the middle ages. Those on display here have not been restored yet their colors remain bright, thanks to the pigments that were used. The blues came from a mineral source (lapis). The gold of the manuscripts is gold leaf held in place with a glue derived from garlic juice. The reds, the curator told us, are extracted from the body fluids of an insect that emerges from the ground in September. She could not give us its name in English. I wondered whether the red pigment was related to cochineal, a dye derived from an insect that lives on New World cactus.*

---

*Later, I found that cochineal was not introduced into Europe until the 16th century, but several related scale insects also produce red pigment. The dye used in the Armenian illuminations apparently came from one of these, an insect, *Porphysophora hamelii*, found in Karabakh. Yet another source of red pigment is the "kermes," a scale insect found as a gall on the kermes oak, *Quercus coccifera*, a bush found in Mediterranean countries and the middle east. European artists used a bright red dye extracted from this source before the introduction of cochineal. Red lead (Pb_3O_4), known as "minium"—from which came our word "miniature" —was also used for early manuscript illumination.

Sunday, 2 August 1993

Armine brought down an "Armenian omelet" for my breakfast. It was delicious. She sautés ripe and juicy tomato slices and two small, hot peppers in butter, and then adds herbs and three eggs. American pink-rock tomato omelet could never be as tasty. After cleaning the apartment, I changed from shorts into long pants. No one wears shorts in Yerevan. It is a prudish city. Now, suitably dressed, I continued with my exploration.

Yerevan was wealthy before the Soviet dissolution; it had the highest density of autos in the USSR. Now there is little traffic. Mike says that Armenian drivers are the worst in the world, not because they are purposely bad, but because no one taught them how to drive. Certainly they are the most inconsiderate drivers I have encountered. If pedestrians are crossing one of Yerevan's wide streets and a car careens around a corner, the driver glares, swerves a bit to avoid the person and honks angrily. Lack of consideration for others may be part of a survival ethos that has kept Armenians and their country alive for three thousand years. To a westerner, however, it is not an admirable trait.

Walking is hot. Every day is sunny and the thermometer outside the apartment usually hits 35º C (94º F) in the shade. It's not as bad as the numbers suggest because the climate is dry and breezy. Early afternoon found me back in the apartment, hungry and dehydrated. I had a lunch of cherries, plums, and apricots from the open market across the street, with bread, cheese, and slices of "bastromah" (cognate with "pastrami," I presume) that Armine brought down. It is dry, shiny, translucent beef, coated with a paste-like rind of brown pepper and garlic—different, but not bad. I opened a can of Polish vodka-and-lemon that I found in a shop the other day. It has an odd taste, but it was good over ice.

My food, except for the little that I buy in the market, or in shops, is cooked by big Ala upstairs. One of the Alas brings it down after I return from work in the late afternoon. Today, big Ala brought meat, fried eggplant and pepper. The eggplant and pepper were good, but the meat was tough and inedible. The meals have been alternating between vegetables, meat and potatoes, and vegetable soups, usually more vegetable than soup. If Ala puts cabbage in her soup it's borscht, otherwise it's just soup.

The other day Abo stopped at a shop on the way back from the hospital. It had wine, the first that I've seen. It is the equivalent of a Greek white barrel wine and it went well with supper. I don't understand why there are so many vines and so little wine in the shops. I suspect that the grapes all go into cognac.

After supper I climbed the tall hill behind our apartment, one of the many that make up a continuous highland around the eastern half of the city. As I climbed, I was surprised to find that Yerevan stretches for miles along the heights. The winters, at the highest elevations, must be really bitter. At the top of the first steep rise, five hundred feet or so above the apartment, I began to feel like an archeologist visiting the ruins of a deserted city, trying to guess the meaning of what I see. There are few people, and many empty buildings. Some, judging by their gaudy signs, are abandoned recreational complexes, restaurants or clubs. When the signs are in Russian, I can usually make out what they say, as the words are similar to English, and the characters bear a distant resemblance to Greek. (The Russian Cyrillic alphabet was derived from Greek uncials.)

A funicular, starting in the city below, ends up here in what seems to have been an amusement park. The cable and cars appear neglected and inoperable. I am continually surprised to see how quickly decay sets in when facilities are not used. Many deserted large buildings appear to have been part of government or military establishments. Four tall steel towers form a square, several hundred yards on each side, connected by an intricate lacework of antenna-like wiring. Is this part of the Soviet space program? Is it used for gathering electronic intelligence? Is it a short wave station? (Later, I asked the doctors about this installation; they knew nothing about it.)

Monday, 2 August 1993

The boxes I shipped from Idaho arrived at the hospital this weekend. They looked as if they had been through hell, although, surprisingly, almost everything arrived safely. The medical supplies went to the OR and the personal items came back to the apartment. I forgot that I'd packed so many things. A real survival trove: brown sugar, cereal, little Hershey bars, instant coffee, peanut butter, Swedish crisp bread (intact!), sleeping bag, stove and fuel, portable printer, batteries, candles, a guide to short wave radio, audio tapes, medical books for the PRSC, and, thankfully, books.

Today was our clinic day. What an assortment of horrors! First, a little girl came in with appalling burn scars of her lower face, neck, chest and back. Her lower jaw is pulled down and almost fixed to her breast bone, she can't close her mouth, her tongue protrudes, and she drools constantly. Surgeons who work with burn patients recognize this as a common type of injury, although usually not so severe. It occurs when a child pulls a container of boiling food, or water, off a stove. The hot material cascades downward, burning the lower face, neck, shoulders and chest. So it was with this little patient. The child should have a tissue expander placed to stretch the skin of her abdomen so we can obtain a large full thickness skin graft to use for reconstructing her neck, but, because her neck cannot be extended, there is no safe way to anesthetize her to put in the expander. This will be a difficult and hazardous procedure.

We also saw a six year old boy who is missing much of his nose. When he was six months old, in his crib, a rat bit it off. We will use a flap from his forehead to replace the missing tissue, the so-called "Indian method." (Noses were amputated in India as punishment for all sorts of offenses. A caste devised this method of reconstruction hundreds of years ago and it is still used today). He was followed by the usual assortment of cleft lips and palates. Some were unrepaired, others need secondary repairs. There were also many patients with hand problems: burns, congenital abnormalities and war wounds. Wan Ho will be busy for the rest of his stay.

Wan Ho came to the States as an immigrant from China after World War II. Otherwise our backgrounds are similar, for we both practiced general surgery for some years before going into plastic and reconstructive surgery. He is an excellent and thoughtful surgeon and I enjoy talking with him.

He is upset about his accommodations, and with some reason. His apartment has water only at unpredictable intervals and then only for an hour or two each day. The electricity also comes on for only a few hours at a time, so he has no light. Further, the electricity and water never come on together, so he has no hot water either. Candles and flashlight are included on the list of items that the AGBU advises volunteers to bring with them, but Wan says he did not receive a list, and he brought neither. He is greatly bothered by the darkness in his apartment, so he has moved into Gagik's office in the hospital, where electricity, light, and water are usually available.*

---

*I discovered that there was more to this than was immediately apparent. Neither Wan Ho, nor I knew that a sixty-eight year old plastic surgeon from Canada had preceded me in Armenia by several months. He died suddenly two weeks after he arrived, while watching television in his apartment—the same apartment assigned to Wan Ho. Gagik found the surgeon dead the next morning.

There were endless problems. Given the circumstances, a postmortem was necessary. It showed, as expected, coronary occlusion. It was a difficult time for Gagik who had to arrange to have the doctor's remains embalmed and prepared for shipment back to Canada. He had to have a coffin made, and lumber was hard to come by in Yerevan and expensive to boot. Gagik then had to arrange

Wednesday, 4 August 1993

This morning we had a free flap scheduled on the man with the electrical burn of the forearm. Wan Ho was to a remove congenital tumor (lymphangioma) of the hand on a nine-months old child in another OR. The parents fed the baby, although they had been warned not to. The infant aspirated stomach contents into her lungs as she was being put to sleep. Nurses and anesthesiologists are supposed to check that patients have taken nothing by mouth before surgery; they did not do so in this case and we came close to losing the child. It would be best if parents did not have access to their kids before surgery, but the doctors say that this would not be acceptable here. At the least, every parent should be told that if they feed their children before an operation, that the child may die. The anesthesiologists were tied up for hours resuscitating the little girl who seems to have recovered without sequelae. By the time this was taken care of it was too late to start the free flap. We went home early.

We are fortunate to have Abo and his van. It would be impossible to get anything done if we had to depend on the city's public transportation. The buses and trolleys are ancient. The buses belch clouds of black diesel smoke (although there are a few with natural gas or propane tanks on their roofs). Passengers, grasping anything that they can get hold of, hang on to the outside of buses and trolleys. Inside, the interiors are jam-packed. It is common to see lines of dead trolleys lined up where an overhead cable has broken, or if the city's electricity fails, as it often does. The passengers wait for a while and then, resigned, give up and walk to wherever they are going.

---

for air transportation. I was told nothing about this incident, and when I finally learned about it, I understood why the AGBU had insisted that I have a checkup before leaving the States.

Back to Wan Ho. One of the AGBU medical personnel in Yerevan ill-advisably told Wan every detail about the doctor's death.

"He was sitting right there in that chair when he died . . ."

This sort of thing bothers me little, but the Chinese feel differently about ghosts of the departed. I suspect that the disclosure of the surgeon's demise had much to do with Wan Ho's relocation to the hospital.

Thursday, 5 August 1993

Something is happening that I don't know about. Gagik is withdrawn, and uncommunicative. Mike McIntyre has been on the phone for hours talking with the AGBU office in New Jersey. Later, Mike asked to meet with me. He told me that friction between the two surgeons has precipitated a crisis. Armine is also involved. I heard Garegin shouting at her several days ago. It seems that the Director, before he left for the States, and without notifying the AGBU, appointed Garegin to be the Chief of the Plastic and Reconstructive Surgical Unit, with the title of "Scientific Director." Unless the staff and the AGBU accept the appointment, Garegin says that he and Tamasian, the Hospital Director, will destroy the Unit.

Garegin's original title was "Director of Medical Education." The title "Scientific Director" has a different connotation. There are nuances of meanings here that are difficult for Westerners to understand. Mike tells me that in Soviet Hospitals, those who bore the title "Scientific Director" were *apparatchiks*, members of the *apparat*, or power structure, whose mission was quality control (translation: "party compliance"). The system was a nasty part of Soviet life bringing petty politics, with graft and corruption, into everyday life. Apparatchiks' positions as party members effectively gave them power over lesser beings who were responsible for day-to-day management and patient care. Garegin is a devout Russophile. He claims that his appointment empowers him to guide the unit and decide policy. Gagik will continue to carry out day to day administration. Mike says—and I suspect that he is right—that Garegin's appointment was designed to stir up trouble. Hospital politics are everywhere, but I have encountered none so strange as this.

[*I was dumbfounded, some weeks later, to learn that the Director announced at a surgical staff meeting that Garegin had paid him to make him the Chief of the PRSC. I asked Armine and Gagik what they thought about this revelation. They shrugged and said in effect that nothing that the Director did surprised them.*]

After Mike briefed me, I met with Gagik and told him that he had my support. The AGBU appointed him Chief and of the two surgeons he is by far the more competent. He is certain that Tamasian is responsible for the present difficulty and is bent on destroying the Plastic and Reconstructive Surgical Center.

"Why would he do such a thing," I asked.

"To get the unit's equipment ." Gagik answered, "then he can do what he wants with it."

Bizarre stories about the Director are unsettling. Last winter, for example, a multi-specialty mission from Columbia University spent two weeks working on the Unit right after it opened. They did many big operations, working in unheated ORS under the most trying conditions. At the end of their stay the visitors gave a party. Some of the Unit's nurses came wearing low-cut American dresses that they had purchased during their year in the States. The Director was shocked by the dresses and angry because he felt that the nurses did not go out of their way to speak to his wife. The next day he fired every one of the Unit's nurses. Some, in time, were reinstated, others were not.

He is said to carry a handgun, and the story goes that he shot a man in his office. The episode was hushed up. On another occasion apparently he saw a man cutting down a tree across the road from the hospital. He opened a window and shot at him.

He has also harassed the Unit's doctors. When it opened, Tamasian told Gagik to deliver all of the Unit's electronic equipment to his office. Gagik refused because the items were supplied by the AGBU (and by the American Agency for International Development). The next day, electricity to the Unit was selectively cut off; the rest of the hospital was unaffected. Power was finally restored, but only after the President of the AGBU called the Armenian Minister of Health. A new movie is playing in the cinema of my mind. Now, I'm one of the humans in *Planet of the Apes*.

I helped Gagik with the free flap that we canceled yesterday. It went well. We used the rectus muscle from the abdomen to fill the forearm defect and covered this in turn with a split thickness skin graft. While Gagik and Leon obtained the muscle, I cleaned up the exposed bone, and exposed the radial artery and a companion vein so we would have vessels to use for restoring circulation to the muscle. Gagik sewed the flap in. He did a good job; the case took only three hours and the flap perfused well from the first.

This afternoon Mike McIntyre met with Garegin and tried to straighten matters out, without success. There are several problems. These include the residual effects of the Soviet system mentioned above, the two surgeon's dislike of each other, and the Unit's need for firm leadership. The last is crucial and Gagik is not providing it.

The Surgical Institute's director seems truly to be malevolent, quixotic and ruthless. He precipitated the present impasse before he left for the States. Mike McIntyre, the American on-site manager, is savvy and has done a superb job in getting this project off the ground. He is not a doctor, however, and is at a disadvantage in dealing with the Director. And then there is the the AGBU in New Jersey, trying to manage things from seven thousand miles away. As a consultant, I'm unsure what my role should be in all this; I may have to intervene.

Friday, 6 August 1993

A quiet day; only two cases. I revised a minor facial scar on the son of the Institute's Director of Radiology. The patient's father has been leaning on Gagik and he, in turn, has been nagging me to do this inconsequential procedure. Our schedule is often slowed or disrupted because physicians prod Gagik to give surgical priority to relatives or friends. Because this is a favor driven society, he must comply.

Our next case was a little girl whose history is much too common. Last winter her father used gasoline to start a fire to heat their house and her clothing caught on fire. She has extensive forearm and groin burn contractures which we released using multiple Z-plasties. (Plastic surgeons often use Z-plasties to release or lengthen tight scars. The technique is difficult to explain, but basically a Z shaped incision is used with the diagonal limb of the Z aligned with the scar. The surgeon then obtains length by transposing the skin flaps that lie between the upper and lower limbs of the Z.)

Saturday, 7 August 1993

Today we drove seventy miles to Gyoumri, Armenia's second largest city, to attend a clinic for earthquake victims. We headed north, paralleling the Arax river. The country slopes gradually downward toward the river, a natural landmark which delineates Armenia's boundary with Turkey. In the river valley, I could see what looked like a nuclear reactor. I asked Gagik about it. Yes, he said, the reactor is located in the little village of Medzamor. It was shut down after the earthquake, although it was not damaged by the tremor.*

On the western (Turkish) side of the river, the land slopes upward to form a massif made up of two mountains. Ararat, the larger of the two, is 17,000 feet (5165 m.) high, irregular and formidable. A smaller, conical

---

*Ongoing border blockade by Azerbaijian and Turkey, and the loss of the Medzamor reactor were the causes of Armenia's acute energy problem. The reactor was shut down in March of 1989, several months after the quake. Two reasons were given. First, was its similarity to the Chernobyl reactor. Second, its location in a seismologically active area. The facility, modernized with Russia's help, was reactivated in the fall of 1995 despite vigorous protests from neighboring nations. Armenia recognized that the reactor is potentially dangerous, but believed that the country's energy needs justified the risk.

sister peak, Little Ararat, rises just to the south. It would be impressive in its own right at nearly thirteen thousand feet, except for its massive neighbor. Ararat lies within the borders of Armenia as they were at the beginning of the century and Armenians still consider it their mountain. As we drove north, I saw another snow-patched peak on our right. It was Mt. Agarats (or Agaracs), the highest mountain within the borders of present-day Armenia. It is made up of four peaks surrounding a volcanic crater over a mile in diameter. The tallest peak is 13,000 feet (4090 m.) high.

Much of northern Armenia is arid, bare, rocky and almost treeless. Wheat grows in the arable areas and animals graze on the rest. The wheat is cultivated by dry farming, as it is in the American west. It is now harvest time, and combines were at work in the fields. Wheat is Armenia's main crop, represented by the lowest band on the country's horizontally striped blue, red, and orange flag.

We saw more abandoned cars that had broken down or run out of gas than there were on the highway. We stopped outside of Gyoumri for a roadside lunch and then drove into the city. Armenian place names are confusing. Gyoumri was known by that name (or by various spelling variants: Goumari, Gumri, etc.) until 1828. Then, when Armenia became part of Russia, its name was changed to Alexandropol. Next, when Armenia became a Soviet state in 1923, the city's name was changed to Leninakin and it was so known in 1988 when the earthquake struck. Finally, after the Soviet breakup, the name reverted to Gyoumri. Today, it is a city of about 70,000 people and still severely scarred from the earthquake. Wood and metal shacks, built from the crates that relief supplies arrived in, are the dominant housing. The outside of many high buildings, all built of the same ubiquitous pinkish tufa, remain, but they have no interiors. Piles of rubble surround the buildings as external perimeters, thrown there by workers searching for victims. The interior collapse of almost every building in Gyoumri was the consequence of Soviet shoddy building methods and materials.

We found forty-five patients waiting for us in a low clinic building. Most were quake victims. Almost all had suffered extremity injuries, characterized by large, severely scarred tissue defects and troublesome amputation stumps. Most of the scar deformities were so extensive that there was little that we could offer. We recommended stump revision for several of the amputees, but most needed only to have their prostheses revised.

An attractive twelve year old girl had bilateral below-the-knee amputations. The stump on the right side was quite short and she had skin breakdown over the residual bone. Despite this, she manages quite well.

We discussed lengthening the remaining bone, but suggested revising her prosthesis first. She appeared, superficially at least, to have adjusted well to her devastating injury. I suspect that it is because so many others have similar deformities. Her's does not set her apart as it might have elsewhere.

A few of the patients had problems unrelated to the quake. One, a nine year old girl, had a large tumor of her shoulder blade which her parents noticed only three months ago. Surgeons in Moscow biopsied it and said that the growth was a "sarcoma." They gave her a few injections of a chemotherapeutic drug and then, for whatever reason, the family returned to Gyoumri before completing her course of chemotherapy. The growth seems localized to the scapula and her mother said that there was no evidence of tumor spread. I am sure that this is an osteogenic sarcoma (a highly malignant tumor of bone commonly seen in the young.) I would have done a scapulectomy, but must admit that the decision not to do so was probably correct. The few osteogenic sarcomas that I have encountered, all of the facial skeleton, had diffuse disease that had spread far beyond the apparent margins of the growth when I operated on them. All died within a few months.

We also saw a teenaged girl who had been operated on in Moscow for a tumor of the orbit (eye socket). She has residual impairment of eye motion and obstruction of her tear duct, probably unavoidable sequelae of her treatment. Neither Wan Ho nor I felt knowledgeable enough to take on the tear duct problem, so we recommended that she return to Moscow for further treatment. Both mother and daughter broke into tears at this point. I tried to explain that American doctors don't know everything, either.

The patients and the hospital staff appreciated our coming, and when we were done, we were served a lunch of cake, candy, fruit, and coffee. The last, to my surprise—given Armenian antipathy to the Turks—is referred to as "Turkish coffee." It, like Greek coffee, is strong, muddy-black, and served in little cups with sludge at the bottom.

Next, we went from the clinic into the hospital proper. It is a substantial older two-story stone building, one of the few structures that survived the earthquake. We met a neurosurgeon, a man who projected an aura of competence. Gagik told us that he was well known for his treatment of combat cranial injuries. He wanted us to see a woman with intractable phantom lower limb pain. Several nerve divisions, and stump revisions had given her no relief. We had little to offer, although she seemed to be suffering from such excruciating pain that I wondered aloud about a cordotomy (severance of pain fibers within the spinal cord). She certainly seemed to be a reasonable candidate for that procedure.

Meanwhile, Marianne had gone to visit the hospital's intensive care unit. She returned with an ICU nurse in tow. Her white uniform was trimmed with dark blue piping and she wore a tall blue paper hat. She is by far the most attractive woman I have yet seen in Armenia. Marianne asked her to pull up her sleeve. Her upper arm was deformed by an enormous, healed defect. She was caught in a building during the earthquake and is missing all of her biceps muscle and the overlying skin.

I asked Armine and Gagik about the quake as we drove back to Yerevan. Their memories were vivid and powerful. It had occurred, they said, at twenty-two minutes to noon. Gagik and Armine's memory differed by three minutes from the official time of nineteen minutes to noon. Many gravestones in Gyoumri have clocks with the latter time carved on them, reflecting the minute at which every clock in the city stopped. I suspect that the three minute difference reflects the gap between the first tremor and the powerful after-shock that did so much damage. At first they didn't know whether it was a mild quake, or a severe one with its epicenter elsewhere. Word of the disaster was slow in coming, for the quake destroyed all communication facilities in Leninakan (Gyoumri) and surrounding areas.

Late in the afternoon, casualties began to arrive in Yerevan, brought in by army trucks. The trucks were so full that the bodies of the injured were packed in, one on top of another. The casualties continued to come in a never-ending procession. Gagik was a young general surgeon then and Armine was a "reanimationist" (the term for an intensivist in the countries of the former USSR. She received her training in anesthesiology during her year in the States). Gagik said that none of the doctors left the Surgical Institute for three weeks. I asked about adequacy of supplies. They said that there were plenty; supplies poured in from all over the world. I questioned Gagik about wound care. Were severe extremity wounds amputated primarily?

"No, none were," he said. "We tried to save every one that we could."

Still, inevitably, many of the injured extremities had to be amputated. It seemed to me, as he described their treatment, that the casualties received excellent care. Open wounds were debrided (cleaned of dirt and dead tissue) thoroughly, and then, properly, were left open to be closed later, when appropriate. The treatment of acute trauma has always been a large part of my surgical practice; nevertheless, it is difficult for me to imagine a disaster of this magnitude.

Our earthquake talk was interrupted when Armine suddenly insisted that we stop. We were in open farm land where wide fields ended at the foot of mountains to the east. Armine wandered off into a wheat field and gathered a bouquet of wild flowers. We resumed our trip. Soon, she again commanded Gagik to stop. She strolled far off into the fields, gathering still another armful of flowers. I could identify wild onion with its ball-like deep purple head, wild thyme, a mallow, and spiny thistles; several others were vaguely familiar. She piled her flowers in the trunk of the car and then left us again, now to visit a donkey tethered in a field, gathering more flowers as she walked along.

I have not asked Armine her age. She is probably about thirty-seven. She is dark-complexioned with thick, jet black hair. Her face is open, with prominent cheekbones. She is taller than the average Armenian woman, full-figured, and she walks with her head held high. She is warm, matter of fact, intelligent and capable. Right now she acts like an uninhibited child as she wanders back and forth in the fields garnering her flowers.

Sunday, 8 August 1993

Armine and little Ala came by and we walked downtown to Republic Square at the city's center. One side of the square is taken up by an impressive building which houses both the National Art and Archaeologic Museums. We visited the art museum first. There was no electricity, but there was enough light from the windows to see fairly well in the outer rooms. Only the works of Armenian artists were displayed; there were many that I would be pleased to own.

The National Archaeologic Museum, on the opposite side of the building, faces Republic Square. Armine recruited a curator to show us around. The lady spoke English and shouted as we went from one exhibit to the next. (Armine had told her that I was hard of hearing, which I am, but not *that* much.) The age and the quality of the artifacts surprised me. The curator told us that metallurgy—the smelting of copper, bronze and iron—may have developed here and the museum has exhibits to support that belief. The displayed artifacts progress step-wise from neolithic times through copper and bronze ages; from obsidian points to bronze spears, arrow-heads and swords. The earliest dated ones are from the fourth millennium B.C. I was also interested to see several nicely crafted wooden wagons. These, more than a thousand years old, had been retrieved from the floor of Lake Sevan after a drop in the water level.

We saw skillfully fashioned, thin-walled clay coffins in which, as in South America, small people were buried sitting up. One finely sculptured woman's head seemed Grecian. The curator said that it represented the Armenian goddess Anahit, the principal deity of pre-Christian Armenia, a divinity analogous to Ishtar (Assyrian and Babylonian), Astarte (Phoenician) and Artemis (Greek). Anahit is a popular girl's name today, usually shortened to Ana. There are many later religious sculptures and carvings including examples of beautifully carved *khachkars* (cross-stones). Many are still found in and around churches, monasteries and other religious sites throughout Armenia.

Republic square would easily hold several football fields. It was a hot day and children paddled in a large pool in front of the museum. The square reminded me of the May Day pictures of Red Square in Moscow, the ones that we used to see on TV and in our news magazines, with thousands of marching soldiers and weaponry. The museum, handsome government buildings, and the impressive Hotel Armenia, line the square on three sides. All are built of a yellow-orange tufa rather than the pinkish brown stone used throughout the rest of Yerevan. A tall unoccupied pedestal dominates the open side of the square across from the museum. Armine explained that Republic square was newly named. It was Lenin Square until the Soviet Union's dissolution. A large statue of Lenin holding a scroll occupied the pedestal. It was toppled and spirited off to who knows where. (Mike later told me that the statue had been sort of a joke anyhow; when viewed from the side, the scroll in Lenin's hand looked like an erect penis.)

Poor Vladimir Ilyich Ulyanov. His cities, squares, and boulevards all have new names. Tree-lined Lenin Avenue ran from the Matenadaran to downtown Yerevan; it is now Mashdot's Avenue (he of the Armenian alphabet.) Lenin's demotion extends throughout all the former Soviet Union. He has been downgraded to a nonentity. Bolshevism failed, but he deserves credit for single-mindedness. He worked to create a form of government that would be right for Russia. Bolshevism, as Lenin envisioned it, was an improvement over Czarist imperialism. He, more than any other person orchestrated the Russian revolution. If its outcome had been as successful as the American revolution, Lenin would still be standing on innumerable pedestals throughout the Soviet Union. In the end it was Lenin's ruthless "democratic dictatorship," that paved the way for Stalin, whose brutal nationalism led eventually to the USSR's downfall. Although they were close friends, Lenin was leery. He felt that Stalin should not be his successor; he was too arbitrary, too rigid. Lenin was right. Unfortunately for Russia, Lenin was rendered ineffective by several strokes, and could not stop the man of steel. Stalin's ruthlessness, paranoia, and drive to export Soviet communism inevitably led first to the Cold War and ultimately to the exhaustion and eventual dissolution of the Soviet Union. So now Lenin, who led the way, is a non-person.

We left Republic Square to walk down to the Razdan River. Everything in Yerevan is "down" or "up" because the city tilts from the heights above the central city down to the river and its ravine. We passed through an older neighborhood where many of the buildings are only two stories high. Some seemed old and date back to the last century or earlier. Armine said that they were in the process of being renovated but the breakup came and the work was never completed. The breakup is a *de facto* reference point for everything in Armenia,.

I wanted to visit a church, for I had seen none in all of Yerevan. Armine pointed out that seventy years of communism had been hell on religion so there are not many churches left. She led us to St. Sarkis, the largest church in the city, overlooking the river gorge. Two christenings were in progress when we arrived, but many other people were there as worshipers. The votive candle business was booming. Candles cost twenty rubles (about two cents to an American, much more to an Armenian) and provide a significant amount of revenue to Armenian churches. We bought our candles and joined the worshipers crowded around one of several sand-filled tables. As I lighted my candles from others burning in the tray, I said a silent prayer. The Armenians crowding around cast sidelong, yet friendly glances in my direction. I am getting used to my alien status.

In spite of Soviet distaste for religion, the state tolerated the Armenian church, although not without a degree of oppression. Now, religion is making a comeback. As we walked back up Mashdots Avenue toward the Matenadaran, Armine pointed to places where other churches had stood before they were razed during the communist era. Although Sunday in Armenia is a day of rest, the shops were open. I wondered whether this failure to honor the Sabbath reflects Soviet influence or, more likely, practical awareness that Sunday is a good day for shopping. I bought two half liter bottles of cognac in a state store. Armenian cognac is fruity and a little sweet. It's easy to drink and I like it, as did Winston Churchill, or so Armenians tell me.

We stopped at a store which Armine said was expensive as it sells mostly imported foods. Nevertheless, the shop was full of customers queuing up to the counter waving handfuls of rubles. I bought two half kilos of cheese: one white, like a hard feta, the other a yellow generic cheese. Both were good. I also bought a long stick of Russian cervelat sausage. This was excellent, the best yet of several kinds of sausage that I've tried here. All of this cost just over 10,000 rubles (about $10). Armenians never fail to ask how prices compare to what we pay in America. I told Armine that the same quantity and quality of cheese and sausage in the US would cost considerably more.

Back in the apartment, as I was relaxing after supper, I received a call from the AGBU office in New Jersey. I learned that the hospital director's position is unequivocally secure. Apparently, even the lady president of the AGBU (whom Mike calls the Empress of Armenia) has tried to have him relieved. Even though he is paranoid, irrational, quixotic and vindictive, he has shaped up the Surgical Institute into a hospital that functions well.

During his stay in the States, the AGBU sent him on a tour of American hospitals. He visited the University of Illinois in Chicago and then went to a hospital in New Jersey, as he wanted to see a facility the same size as the Surgical Institute. He was impressed, evidently, with what he saw and he wants to inaugurate reforms; same day in-and-out surgery, for example. The AGBU's representative was optimistic and felt that we would be dealing with a new, made-over Director. Gagik, who knows him best, looks sad whenever we talk about him.

"He's very, very bad," Gagik says about the Director. "He will fool them. He will not change."

Next, we discussed the still unresolved Garegin affair. I said that if the AGBU wished, I would become involved. They agreed, and said that the AGBU wants Garegin demoted. Garegin's title will then be "Surgeon," period. No more "Scientific Director" nonsense. We discussed a few other matters, with satisfactory resolutions to most. Whether these will be valid after the Director's return remains to be seen. All who know Tamasian believe that he will revert to status quo the instant he feels Armenian soil beneath his feet.

Later, Armine came down with a half loaf of bread fresh from the oven, still steaming. We ate thick slices with butter melting over the hot bread, and drank cognac on ice. She knew I had been expecting the call. I told her about our conversation. Armine shook her head when I told her about the Director.

"He'll never change," she said in a very small voice, echoing what Gagik had said earlier. The doctors and others take a dim view of the AGBU's campaign to reform Tamasian. Armine also brought down a transformer for my portable printer. It doesn't work with the local current. With her transformer it did work—for three lines. Then it auto-cremated with heat, smoke, bad smell and melting plastic. At least I won't have to schlepp it back to the States.

Monday, 9 August 1993

Today I did two cleft palates with Garegin. They went well. Next we adjusted the cross lip flap that we did last week. The border of the lip was off. I'm not sure how this happened, except that the lip was so badly scarred that it was difficult to see landmarks during last week's surgery.

Because this was also our day to see patients, we got a late start in the OR and didn't finish until early evening. Even though it was late, I wanted to meet with Garegin and get that out of the way. We met in his office. I told him that we'd had enough of his nonsense. Gagik, I said, is absolutely and unequivocally chief of the Unit. Garegin tried to argue, but I replied that *I* represented the AGBU and whatever I told him was the way that things will be. Repeatedly and forcefully I said that he is not and will not be the Unit's chief. He is another surgeon, period. I also suggested that he make peace with those whom he has alienated, Armine especially. I doubt however, that he will be able to bring himself to do that.

Eventually, he agreed to everything. He ended by saying that the only reason that he was making trouble was because he could not get cases assigned to him. This is baloney. He has never wanted to do the larger cases. Nevertheless, as a sop, I promised that I would look into the matter. Patient assignment *is* a problem, although I am not sure that anything can be done about it. Gagik gets the interesting cases. Other physicians know him, like him, and refer patients directly to him. Garegin sits in his office with the door closed and shows little interest in doing anything, other than cleft lips and palates.

In any event, I hope that the immediate problem is solved and that matters can go on smoothly from now on— although Director's impending return does engender a degree of apprehension.

Tuesday, 10 August 1993

This morning we operated on the little girl with the gunshot wounds of her forefoot. We used the small abductor muscle to the great toe on one side of her foot and a skin flap on the other to give good soft tissue coverage of both wounds. Next, I did an extensive reconstruction on a bilateral cleft lip nose. (Cleft lip deformities often involve more than the lip. The nose and the facial skeleton are also effected, sometimes so severely that nasal reconstruction is a greater problem than the lip.)

After we finished, Gagik and I sat down to talk. I told him that he must work to organize the unit and—most importantly—he had to start acting like a chief. I'm afraid, however, that his greatest problem will be his distaste for organization and detail, rather than a lack of assertiveness.

This evening the AGBU called again, this time to ask about my meeting with Garegin. I told them that he now seems willing to cooperate. I don't know how sincere he is; time will tell. They are trying to manage the Unit by overseas telephone without realizing that it just won't work. They are dealing with shadows and know only what people tell them on the phone. No one from the organization has been here, apparently, since work on the Unit began, nor have any of the medical consultants who were involved in the planning, staffing, and equipping the Unit been in Armenia since an initial visit.

Thursday, 12 August 1993

Our first case today was a Z-plasty to release a burn contracture of the popliteal space (the area behind the knee) on a burned child. Next, we operated on a little paraplegic lady with "myelitis." She had a large sacral decubitus ulcer over the sacrum. (Decubitus ulcers are sores that form in areas where bony prominences lie close to the skin: typically ankles, hips, and sacral region of the back. They commonly occur in paraplegics and others confined to bed for lengthy periods of time.)

Patient diagnoses here are bewildering. Myelitis, for example, is a catch-all term for an inflammatory condition of the central nervous system, but beyond that it has little diagnostic meaning, so I have don't know the cause of this patient's paraplegia. Yesterday, we saw a man with tumors of his hands and arms who came in with a diagnosis of "podagra." My clinical impression was that the man had gout. Then I remembered that "podagra" is an old word for gouty inflammation of the big toe. Here, the word apparently means any kind of gout.

A lack of a meaningful diagnosis can adversely effect patient care. We now have an old man with an ulceration which has destroyed much of his right face. Both Wan Ho and I are certain that it is a squamous cell carcinoma, a common cancer of the skin, lip, mouth, throat, sinuses and lungs, often related to sun exposure (skin and lip) or to smoking. Two previous biopsies have showed only "inflammation." Three days ago, I did a very generous biopsy. The pathologists here in the hospital again report only "inflammation." I am unwilling to excise half his face without a documented tissue diagnosis of malignancy. Fortunately, the pathologists sent some of the tissue to the Yerevan Oncology Hospital. The pathologists there say that the man's tumor is an "epithelioma," another non-specific diagnosis, but at least it is consistent with squamous cell carcinoma, so we'll go ahead with surgery.

The paraplegic lady with myelitis has had many pressure sores. Gagik successfully closed a large ulcer on her hip six weeks ago. Today, we covered an enormous sacral ulceration using bilateral gluteal muscle flaps. These worked well, but she bled profusely during the procedure. The blood appeared thin and watery. It turned out that Armine, expecting that the patient would lose a lot of blood, had pre-hydrated her with a generous infusion of Ringer's lactate solution. Armine said that it wasn't really blood that was flowing out as we worked, it was just the Ringer's lactate. Nevertheless we arranged for a transfusion at the end of the case. She needed it. Otherwise, the procedure went well and the flaps have good circulation.

This evening I called a former associate, Dr. Catherine Vlastou, in Athens, to ask her if she would volunteer to come to Armenia for a week or two. We had been closely associated in practice for many years before she was forced by family problems to return to Athens. She is the most meticulous surgeon I know. The Armenian surgeons would benefit from working with her, and we could do microsurgical cases that I'm reluctant to take on alone. She will consider it and let us know. Wan Ho has left us, but another volunteer plastic surgeon arrives tomorrow.

Friday, 13 August 1993
No surgery this morning. Mike McIntyre and the surgeons have gone to the airport to pick up a new volunteer from the States, Dr. Daniel De La Pava from Phoenix, Arizona.

Saturday, 14 August 1993
Saturday is my day for deep cleaning. Staying ahead of Yerevan grime is a challenge. The pollution settles as a black gritty deposit. Because it's so hot, I leave the doors and windows open. and dust all surfaces every day. When I see how much falls on shiny surfaces, I know that it also accumulates where I can't see it, on rugs, furniture, curtains, bedding—everywhere. The soles of my white socks turn gray if I take even a few steps without shoes.

This evening Armine, little Ala and I walked downtown to the Yerevan Metro; I never cease to be surprised at things this city has. We went down to the Metro station on the steepest, fastest and longest escalator I've ever seen. The plastic fare tokens cost ten rubles each, about a cent. The Metro is modern and compares favorably with those of London or Paris, although here there is only one line. Its architecture is Soviet contemporary, with marble throughout. The stations are clean and there is no advertising and no graffiti. The trains are fast and capacious. Armine says that the Yerevan Metro is a duplicate of the the Moscow system. The difference is that here passengers must know exactly when the trains will run, or else, when the power is turned off, they will be stranded far from home. We rode for two stations and then walked down to the Razdan river and crossed on a high bridge over the ravine. Below, the river ran white in the depths of the gorge.

On the far side, we entered a large park with paved paths. After walking for a quarter of a mile, we came to to the Genocide Monument, a holy place for Armenians. It consists of thirteen massive, inwardly leaning, squarish stone columns which nearly meet at the top to form a dome. Each one represents a region in Anatolia where the Turks massacred upwards of one and a half million Armenians in 1915 and 1916 in what was this century's first genocide. Inside, there is a large bronze centerpiece which, in better times, has an eternal flame.

"Who still talks of the Armenians?" Hitler asked in defending the Nazi slaughter of Jews. We can answer Hitler's question; millions of Armenians still think and speak of their genocide. It has become part of their collective memory. Those who descend into the monument—many bringing bouquets of flowers—are clearly deeply moved. The Armenians say, along with the Jews with whom they identify, that they are determined that such a thing will never again happen.

A tall four-sided stainless steel needle, representing today's Armenia, stands next to the monument. Early in the morning, when it reflects the rising sun, I see this from my balcony on the other side of Yerevan, although until now I did not know what it was. There are many fountains nearby. None are working, although the gardens lining the walks are being maintained. A sculpture of agonal bodies backs one of the garden plots.

As we turned back toward the river, a wide walkway led past a concert hall that reminded me of the much-pictured opera house that overlooks the harbor in Sydney, Australia. This one is an enormous building, with concave white roofs soaring upward like wings and massive stone ramps leading to its entrances. Altogether, it is a remarkable structure, although now in disrepair. The many cusps and valleys of its roof can be seen from all over the city.

We took a minibus back to the Metro. By now it was nearly dark and Armine was glad to return, as the unlighted streets seem menacing to her. It is not uncommon to hear gunfire in the night. Marianne says that she heard automatic fire in the streets almost nightly last winter. Nocturnal gunfire is one of Yerevan's mysteries. Do people shoot at each other, fire into the air, or are they engaging in target practice?

I am more bothered by the nightly concert of dogs than I am by the shooting. One dog barks, others answer. Once started, the canine concert goes on all night. Like the gunfire, the barking stops at dawn. The dogs, I am told, have reverted to their lupine heritage; they form packs and attack people, children especially. It seems strange that there are so many stray dogs in a city with so many shortages. Where do they scavenge their food? They can't all be subsisting on the occasional human.

Sunday, 15 August 1993

We went today to Lake Sevan for what Gagik termed an "Armenian Barbecue." Sevan lies forty miles east of Yerevan. The lake is Armenia's dominant geographic feature although it has diminished in size in recent years, thanks to Soviet "improvements" that dropped the lake's water level considerably. The engineers devised a project to obtain more land for agriculture and water for hydroelectricity by draining the lake through underground tunnels. Despite this meddling, it is still plenty big, nearly thirty miles wide and fifty miles long.

Andrei Bitov, a Russian author, described Armenia as a country characterized by three singularities: A city (Yerevan), a lake (Sevan) and a mountain (Ararat), ignoring the actuality of the mountain's location. Armenia managed to keep the city and the lake. Sevan is an important resource. The Razdan river, its natural outlet, supplies power. The lake provides the only fresh fish available to Armenians. Finally it is popular for recreation, although now, because of hard times, few are able to visit.

We left Yerevan in several cars. Gagik's car was overloaded. Gagik and I were in front. Gagik's wife Gohar and their two boys along with Armine, and little Ala were all squeezed into the back. We made several stops: for firewood, for melons, and for a great roll of lavash, the traditional flannel-like Armenian flat bread. Finally, we were on our way. Gagik picked up speed and we moved along with the speedometer needle squarely on 100 Km (62 mph.) Then, as we descended a long hill, a rear tire exploded. The car held steady for a second and then lurched. I experienced an adrenal-contracting, gut-wrenching, no seat belt, helpless, "this is it," flash as the car slewed back and forth. Gagik finally managed to get it under control and brought us to a stop on the shoulder. I silently gave thanks that it hadn't been a front tire. He has had never ending problems with tires. We had a flat as we drove back from Gyoumri. He had another at the airport, and yet another in Yerevan. He replaced all four tires with new ones. One of these blew out now. As Gagik removed the shredded tire and mounted a spare, I had time to reflect on the pervasive shoddiness with which these people live. We resumed our trip, although more slowly. As we crested a low hill, I saw Lake Sevan spread out before us, reaching all the way to the horizon.

The lake is striking. It is surrounded by moderately high, treeless mountains. The flanks of the higher ones are still, even in mid-August, covered with patches of snow. The lake is an incredible light turquoise, a color more commonly seen in tropic seas. A train station, a few hotels and several restaurants stand close to the shore. They are all in the Soviet-modern style, an exaggeration of the art deco architecture popular in the States during the 1930s. Two stone churches stand on a hillside overlooking the lake. Originally built on an island, they are now on a peninsula, thanks to human meddling with the water level. A line, well above the shore, on the steep slopes of the island/peninsula show where the original shoreline was.

We established a base in some low trees by the uncrowded beach, started a fire, and then swam in the cold water. The beach and lake floor are sandy, and that, I presume, is what gives Sevan its turquoise color. It was now early afternoon, so we broke out lunch. Big Ala's piroshki (meat and rice cooked into a pastry covering), sausage, cheese and lavash. Gagik had bought yards and yards of lavash tightly rolled into a cylinder about a foot in diameter and eighteen inches wide. This unleavened Armenian bread is cooked just enough to brown it, so it is limp and very thin. Lavash looks and feels like thickish cloth, and is rather like a flour tortilla in consistency, but thinner. It has many uses. It is ideal for wrapping around cheese, sausage, or any other filling. It serves as a napkin or as a plate. It is perfect for mopping up the last bit of food, and it tastes good. We might import piroshki and lavash from Armenia to the States, to our mutual benefit.

After lunch we played soccer on the beach. Like most older Americans, I've never played, but to Armenians it's an all-important sport, the equivalent of baseball and football combined; it is a sport that they grow up with. As we kicked the ball back and forth, we were joined by visitors. Every one else on the beach had parked their car—tired old Ladas, Volgas, Moskvas, and Zaporozets—behind a marginal road that runs well above the shoreline. Now, a deep maroon, shiny, showroom new BMW nosed aggressively down onto the sand, to park at the water's edge. Then an equally new, sparkling white Jeep Wrangler pulled in beside the bimmer. These two brand new cars had to arrive in Armenia by air; there is no other way to get them into the country.

A man and four women stepped out of the vehicles. The women were fashion caricatures. One wore a frou-frou white dress with ruffles over its entire surface. Another, younger and more attractive, wore stylish little black pantaloons, open at the sides and tied with bows at her ankles; beneath these she wore a modish bathing suit. A third woman showed off smart, tight-fitting white stirrup slacks, and a chic little toreador blouse. The fourth woman was older. She had dyed platinum blond hair and wore a flouncy pink and white little girl's dress with a flaring skirt. She led a tiny dog on a long leash. A paunchy, black-haired man was master of this entourage. The man, his automobiles, his harem, their exaggerated fashions,were as out of place on this beach as jackals at a dog show. I turned to Gagik

"Who *are* these people?" I asked.

He made an eloquent, disgusted face.

"They're nothing." he said. "They only make show. A little while they had nothing."

"Where did all their sudden money come from?" I queried.

"Maybe bring things in, make lots of money." He shrugged. "I don't know."

He turned away. Clearly he did not care to discuss the matter further. A little while later, the dog escaped from its mistress, and ran down the beach. I stepped on its leash as it ran past me, and led the animal back to its owner. She was expressionless, her powdered face white as a mime's except for bright red lips and two blotches of sharply demarcated rouge smeared across her cheekbones. I handed her the dog's leash. Total indifference. She said nothing, took the leash and walked languidly back to her car. Such was my introduction to Armenia's nouveau riche, the Mafia. They are who we see in Yerevan, driving new, air-lifted Jeep Cherokees, Mercedes, BMWs, and Volvos.

While I was watching the fashion show, Karen Manvelyan arrived. He is the Unit's second anesthesiologist, now back from vacation in Belarus. He wore a deep blue T-shirt with four white Cyrillic characters written boldly across the front. I asked him to translate. "Yale," he said, purchased while the Armenians were in New Haven.

Later, Karen took us to visit the church of the Apostles and the church of the Virgin Mary on the peninsula. As we left the parking lot to follow the path up to the churches, I noted that two shrubs at the base of the trail were covered with tied-on pieces of cloth. This custom is common throughout the country, seen mostly near religious sites.

The two Sevan churches stand together on the sometime island, just below the brow of a central hill. They are the only remaining buildings in what was originally a sizeable monastery complex. Now, only crumbling foundations of the other buildings remain. Both churches have cruciform floor plans, and each has a high multi-faceted central dome. The interiors of the domes are similar to those seen in ancient Greek churches, at Daphne near Athens, or Mistra near Sparta on the Peloponnesus. The Armenian churches, however, lack the stern Pantocrater whose figure fills the dome, right hand raised in blessing. The Greek orthodox iconostasis completely separates clergy and congregation during the Eucharist, whereas the iconostasis in Armenian churches is represented by icon-like paintings along the front of a raised dais.

The Sevan churches were built in 874 A.D., commissioned by Miriam, a Siuniq Princess. (Siuniq was a principality that lay east of Ararat and south along the Arax river as far as Zangezour in southern Armenia. It included Lake Sevan within its borders. Tradition has it that the Siuniqs adopted Christianity and that there were even Siuniq bishops, well before Armenia itself converted to Christianity during the first years of the fourth century. Its name persists today as a precinct south of Sevan.) The pinkish brown tufa of the exterior walls is weather beaten, but intact. It seems strange to be looking at functioning Christian churches this old.

I bought five candles and added them to ones burning in the sand trays while thinking a prayer for family and friends. The candles gave off a pervasive and not unpleasant odor of burning beeswax. Smoke filled the churches with a haze so thick that the shafts of sunlight entering through the little windows beneath the high dome appeared solid.

The Sevan churches with their conical exterior domes are typical of early Armenian church architecture. The stonework domes differ from those seen in Europe and apparently were constructed using a technique devised earlier. Armenian churches are far smaller than the later European ones, and so, presumably, the architectural problems of gravity-defying stone-built domes were more easily solved. The preservation of these two churches, in this volatile part of the world, can be explained by an unbroken seventeen centuries of Armenian Christianity on one hand, and by their island inaccessability on the other.

When we returned to our base, the fire had burned down. Eggplants, tomatoes, and green peppers, skewered on swordlike spits, lay across iron rails above the glowing coals. The women's hands were black from removing charred skin from roasted eggplants. Tomatoes and peppers, charred more lightly, were put in large bowls lined with lavash. The men now threaded gobbets of pork, marinated overnight with onions and peppers, onto the skewers to roast over the coals. Dripping fat served as fuel and kept the coals glowing. A dense column of white smoke rose and democratically blew here and there to engulf hungry onlookers. The men tended to the meat meticulously, cutting into each piece of pork to be certain that it was well cooked. As the meat browned, the cooks slid it off the skewers into big lavash lined bowls. I found it hard to believe that even such a large party as ours could eat this enormous bounty of meat. The cooks reassured me. We could.

A tight ring of eaters formed around the full bowls. Chinks between eaters were filled with cheese, with cups for the grownups' vodka and the children's tonic, with cold cuts of sausage, and with big piles of lavash. No spoons, forks, or knives; fingers only. Back to basics. The barbecue was delicious. The pork was roasted to perfection, crispy, tender, and tasty.

"I like better than American barbecue, do you?" Gagik asked.

Apples and oranges; both are delicious in their own way, particularly when eaters are hungry. We pigged out, an appropriate term for that meal. It was pig all the way. And we ate it all. Everything. The pork, the ripe cooked tomatoes, charred pepper, slippery eggplant, the ragged sheets of juicy lavash that lined the bowls. Raw vodka, served in paper cups, cut the fat. Afterward we topped off with chunks of melon and big slices of watermelon. I don't know what name to give the melon; it was closest to our honeydew, but heavier, riper and sweeter. The watermelon was also perfect, ripe and sweet, filled with brilliant red seeds.

Obviously "Armenian barbecue" is a convenient English term for an ancient rite which originated, I suspect, with animal sacrifice. The men knew exactly what they were about. They told me that they had learned from their fathers, who had, in turn, learned from their fathers before them—and so on back through time. If I felt the need for an Armenian Barbecue I would never attempt to emulate the meal that we had at Lake Sevan. I'd find Armenian men to do it.

Thankfully, the trip back to Yerevan was uneventful. We traveled together now, for our three cars had had three flats between them and there were no spare tires left. We stopped once. Gagik had brought bottles with him and he wanted to get water from a roadside spring. As he filled his containers, Karen, Marianne and I hunted for the perfect specimen of obsidian. Obsidian is scattered all over Armenia. It is shiny, black as coal, and fractured into odd shapes. The black quartz is a natural glass that is found in outcroppings, on the surface of the ground, and throughout the soil. Obsidian is easy to work. Prehistoric peoples used it for their points: arrows, knives, axes, spears, and the like, before bronze and iron were available.

Other cars stopped for water, and their passengers also wandered about collecting the shiny stones. I have seen it used for doorstops, paper weights, jewelry, candlesticks, and bookends. It is a decorative mineral. The glistening, black stones are a dividend, a perk, a minor compensation, for living in a bleak land.

Back in Yerevan, Armine, little Ala and I climbed slowly up the stairs to our apartments. We were sunburned, full, and happy. It had been a good day. The "starving Armenians" that the children of my generation were told about are, in spite of today's troubles, doing pretty well.

Monday, 16 August 1993

Today is clinic day. Between patient visits we reconstructed the rat-bitten child's nose using a flap from his forehead. The boy has a very low forehead and the flap is covered with downy hair, although that will disappear as he ages. We will divide its connection with his forehead in a couple of weeks.

Tuesday, 17 August 1993

We operated on the elderly man with the cancer of his face. The growth is so extensive that I couldn't tell where it began. It may have started in the skin and eroded into the mouth and jaw, or more likely, it originated in his mouth, or sinus. I resected it, without benefit of a pathologist's frozen sections, without usable x-rays and without a CT scan. We had sent him for a CT scan, but when I asked for the films I learned that there were none. There is only one CT scanner in Yerevan. The radiologist reads directly from the monitor screen because the hospital has no film to record the findings. That may be OK for diagnostic studies in other parts of the body, but it is not much help for the head and neck surgeon. Although we spared his eye, we removed most of the rest of the right side of his face. I think that we were around the cancer, but I would have been happier if we'd had frozen section control. The defect was enormous, We used a skin flap from his chest to cover it. The operation took most of the day.

Afterwards, as we relaxed in the lounge in Gagik's office, I asked Karen Manvelyan about the Armenian police system. Armenia is a police state. Not as Nazi Germany was, but rather as a country overrun by policemen. Traffic police are everywhere in Yerevan and along the main roads leading out of the city. We had seen many on our trip to Sevan. They set up roving checkpoints consisting usually of five or six officers, and two or three police cars. One officer stands in the road and randomly points a baton at a passing car, signalling its driver to pull over. Another policeman then checks the driver's papers and searches for minor vehicular violations. He usually finds one. Rubles change hands on the spot. If the driver is unable to pay his fine, the police confiscate his license (I say "his" advisedly. I have yet to see a woman driver in Armenia.) In this event, to retrieve his license the driver must present himself at the central police station where he pays an even larger fine. The traffic police often stop Abo as he drives around the city on hospital errands. Most recently they cited him because some paint had peeled away from his van's license plate. Not having enough cash for the instant payoff, Abo surrendered his license. He then spent his afternoon at the police station. It cost 15,000 rubles (currently about $15 American, or one to two weeks pay, Armenian) to recover his license.

Random extortion of this sort is a dirty game of Monopoly where, according to the roll of the dice, players land on penalty squares and pay with real money. The implications of such pervasive police harassment bothers me. It is left over from the Soviet era. A universal police presence does not bode well for any country's future.

"You know," Karen said as we talked about this, "you come here and you see things, but it is hard to explain them to you in such as way that you will understand our system."

He went on to tell me that the police were checking for criminals, stolen cars, etc., and that they were therefore filling a necessary function.

"That's all to the good," I said, "but what does that have to do with harassing drivers and extorting money on any pretense?" He answered only with a shrug. I wanted to talk further with him, but the ICU called just then to ask us to come to see our patient, because he looked pale. There was no problem. We reassured the nurses and headed for home.

It has been a month since I left Idaho. I am lonely, and was happy to talk to Barbara this evening. Cathy Vlastou, my former associate in Athens, also called. She is willing to come for a week. That will help. We should be able to get a few big cases out of the way during her stay.

Thursday, 19 August

Today I helped Gagik operate on a soldier wounded in Karabakh. He had a massive bone and soft tissue defect which involved the upper two thirds of the tibia and surrounding soft tissues. When we first saw the patient a week ago on the Orthopaedic Service, the wound was too grungy to work with. It has cleaned up with daily saline dressings and we were able to go ahead with his surgery today. I recommended a latissimus muscle free flap from his back, although the injury is so extensive that it might be difficult to find suitable recipient vessels to attach it to, so vein grafts might have been needed. Gagik asked about transposing the gastrocnemius muscle from behind his leg and using that to cover the defect. I was sure that the muscle had been injured by the gunshot, and I doubted that it would be suitable. Further, if we use the gastroc we would also have to use the adjacent soleus muscle, because the wound is so extensive. The two muscles, used together, just might work, although at the cost of functional impairment.

We presented both alternatives to the patient and to the orthopaedists. The soldier didn't want to have a muscle removed from his back, so we used the adjacent muscles from his calf. Both muscles were bloodshot, but in better condition than I expected and we were able to use them to cover the whole defect. We decided not to skin graft the exposed muscles today as they are under some tension, but will return in a few days and put split-thickness skin grafts on them.

The orthopaedists watched us as we did the surgery and were delighted with the result. I asked how they would fill in the huge bony defect. No problem, they said. They would use the "Ilizarov technique." First they would shorten the whole leg six inches until the residual bone ends meet. When these are healed they will divide the bones above and below the defect and stretch the leg back to length again. This is done slowly—a millimeter or two a day—so that the divided tibia and fibula make new bone as they are stretched. My skepticism showed, but they assured me that the technique would work. I am impressed with what these orthopaedists are able to do using the method. Our orthopaedic surgeons are just starting to use the Ilizarov technique in the States. They might be interested to see how it is done here and its results.

Friday, 20 August 1993

No surgery today. Everyone went to the airport to meet two American nurses who arrived this morning. One, Jayne Prentice, will be in charge of the OR. She was a Navy nurse in Vietnam so she should feel at home here. The other, Ingrid Lusko, will be nurse manager. She will take over from Mike who is leaving in a few days for the States.

Saturday, 21 August 1993

Armine came down early and we crossed the street to the outdoor farmers' market across from our apartment. The stalls were filled with piles of eggplant, tomatoes, bunches of coriander, basil, parsley, and dill, peaches, melons and other produce. Armine says that I should not come here alone, because I am an American and I am congenitally unable to bargain. The only reason that I can see for the persistence of bargaining, is that occasionally some person—most likely an alien like myself—chances along and pays a price that the seller asks.

The transactions go like this: The vendor states a price, say one thousand rubles for a kilo of produce: melon, eggplant, fruit, whatever. Armine considers this briefly and then makes an unhappy face. She counters with six hundred rubles. The final price is eight hundred which both knew it would be in the first place. A few sellers won't bargain. If Armine likes their produce and the price is fair, she buys. If not, she walks on to the next stall. When a price is agreed on, she carefully picks the fruit or vegetables that she wants. Her selection is then put in a pan, and weighed on a balance scale. The buyer provides the container, so Armenian women always carry plastic bags, a practice that pays off if a bargain turns up anywhere on the street.

Finally, there is the business of paying. The vendors never seem to have change, although in the end they always find it. I started to make a gesture to forget the last ten rubles of change as a vendor was having more than the usual amount of trouble. Armine stopped me.

"Armine, ten rubles are less than a penny." I said, as we walked back across the street.

"I know," she said, "but it's not a penny in Armenia. My monthly salary from the hospital, in rubles, is less than twenty American dollars. Ten rubles is a lot here."

Dr. Dan De La Pava is our plastic surgeon of the month. He laughs whenever he hears Armine telling me about what I must or must not do.

"She acts just like your wife." he says.

This evening, Gagik came by to take us to a dinner to honor Mike McIntyre whose departure is imminent and whose birthday is today. We went to the "Big Mafia Restaurant," so-called because only mafia can afford to eat there. There were ten of us: Mike McIntyre and his wife Sue, Gagik and his wife Goharik, Dan De La Pava, the two new American nurses Jayne and Ingrid, Marianne Hess, Karen Manvelyan, Armine and me. Garegin was not in the company. I don't know whether that was his choice, or because he wasn't invited and I didn't ask.

The dinner started off awkwardly, but matters improved quickly, for Mike had received a bottle of German vodka as a present. He passed it around. Then we bought another bottle of French vodka. Its brand name was "Boris Jelsen." The French seem to be keeping up with the political situation, vodka-wise. Our glasses stayed full. Mike was toasted first and then each guest in turn. I tried to keep up with Armine who seems to have a hollow leg. I asked her how we are going to get up five flights of stairs to our apartments.

"Don't worry," she said. "We'll help each other."

Fortunately the vodka was buffered by hors d'oeuvres. Dry cervelat, crisp fried meat and pastry rolls, greens (cooked and raw), big caper berries, caviar and cream cheese, yogurt (more sour and less processed than ours, but good), green and black olives, sliced tomatoes and cucumbers, bread (coarse Armenian bread and thin lavash), bastromah, and "sutsuki," another dried meat.

Karen Manvelyan told me that drinkers in Armenia say "gay-nah-SEHDT," a salute that does not mean "to your health," as in other countries. Rather, it means "survive," with overtones of ". . . and flourish." Armenians feel that that sentiment is right for them. Karen believes that Jews have a similar toast and listed many similarities between Jews and Armenians. Both groups are survivors, he said. Meals such as this have a ritualistic, toasting etiquette. One person, the host, or the most prominent person—Gagik in this case—is the *tamada* ("tama-DAH", a Georgian term that evidently is used throughout the former Soviet world for a banquet's toastmaster. Toasts are offered in order according to the importance of the guests, so Mike was first today. No one is neglected. Other guests may give toasts, after asking the tamada's permission. After all the diners have been recognized, anything goes: women, children, friendship, international relations, and on and on for as long as the vodka and the guests hold out.

Our next course, the house specialty, was beef soup in individual ceramic pots, topped with a thick baked crust. Then spiced sausages with fried potatoes and mushrooms. Boris Jelsen was our constant companion; the toasts never stopped. For dessert there was generic ice cream topped with blackberries, and Turkish coffee. The waiter brought three long-stemmed roses for each lady, a nice touch. Armine told me that Armenians always give odd numbers of flowers in social settings. It would be unlucky to do otherwise for even numbers are reserved for death and funerals.

The two new American nurses and Dan De La Pava were enjoying themselves at the other end of the table. I got a good look at our new recruits for the first time. Ingrid is a slim, outgoing, middle aged, blonde lady with frizzy hair obscuring her upper face. She could pass for Michelle Pfeifer's older sister. Jayne is tiny, a micro-nurse who sat quietly through dinner.

Gagik in this setting is natural and seems humble. In the hospital he is bluff and preoccupied, but tonight he is outgoing. His English is basic, yet he gets his meaning across clearly, even as he gropes for English words. When he does, Armine translates or fills in. She is the reason, Gagik says, that he cannot speak English well.

Toward the end of the evening, Dan De La Pava quietly snuck out and picked up the tab. It seemed a lot for him to do, and he refused my help. On our way home Gagik asked me how much I thought the dinner cost, including three bottles of Boris Jelsen vodka, roses for the ladies, music and tips. I guessed three or four hundred dollars. Ninety dollars, Gagik said. He wanted to know how much our dinner would have been in America. I told him that one couple could easily spend that much and more in a good restaurant. There are advantages for those who visit Armenia bearing dollars.

And so back to the apartment where no one had to help anyone up the stairs. Vodka, even when consumed in such large amounts, is buffered with food. A social glow results, rather than inebriation, a better way than our foodless, preprandial cocktail gatherings.

Sunday, 22 August 1993

Gagik came by at 11:00 a.m. with Dan De La Pava, Jayne and Ingrid. He says that we are going to visit a "pagan temple."

We drove up and out of the city, then through winding mountain roads to Guarni, the site of an ancient fortress and a small temple. The temple dates to the time of King Tiridates I who ruled Armenia during the second half of the first century, A.D. Seemingly, because of its perfection, the structure was spared when Armenia became Christian in the fourth century, a time when other pagan buildings were destroyed or cannibalized to build churches for the new religion. The temple fell in an earthquake in 1629, then was excavated and rebuilt by archeologists in the 1960s. It is a perfect little Greco-Roman temple supported by twenty four columns with intricately carved Ionic capitals. There is an altar in the rear where the walls are blackened, presumably by the smoke of sacrifices.

The ruins of a palace are nearby, including the mosaic floor of a bathhouse. I had already seen a reproduction of the mosaic in the museum in Yerevan. It is decorated with fish and has Greek writing around its periphery which in the museum is translated as "We labored for no reward." I wonder if Greek slaves laid the mosaic floor and added the lettering, secure in the knowledge that it would be Greek to their masters? Cliffs on three sides fall away into a lush green valley. The temple and the royal complex stand on the highest point, a mini-acropolis for uncertain times.

From Guarni we drove to the nearby Gekhard monastery. Gekhard means "spear" in Armenian, a reference to the spear that pierced Jesus' side, a relic that was kept here, but has been removed to the museum of the cathedral in Echmiadzin, the seat of the Armenian Apostolic (Orthodox) church. The monastery lies below a hanging valley in rugged, mountainous terrain. A cobbled walk leads up to the monastic complex. Vendors along the walkway sell roosters and pigeons for animal sacrifice, a practice still very much alive in Armenia. I told Gagik that I wanted to sacrifice a cock. He gave me a look of disgust. Not all Armenians hold the practice of live sacrifice in high regard.

The story of how animal sacrifice was incorporated into the Armenian church's ritual is interesting. In the pre-Christian era, priesthoods were dynastic, and animal sacrifice was a paramount part of their religion. It was also a perquisite, a source of food for the priests and their families. On learning that Christianity did not require animal sacrifice, pagan priests sent an envoy to Tiridates III (Trdat the Great, 287-330 A.D.) the first Christian ruler of Armenia.

"[They] asked him how they were to live if they became Christians, for until then the priests and their families depended on the animal offerings reserved to them by pagan custom. [They were told that] if they would join the new religion, not only should the sacrifices continue, but they should have larger perquisites than ever. The priestly families converted en masse." (Frederick Cornwallis Conybeare, M.A., D.Th., *Encylopedia Britannica*, 11th Ed. vol 2, page 569, 1910-11)

Thus, animal sacrifice was incorporated into the Armenian Church's eucharistic rites. In the sacrificial ritual, the wreathed victim is made to lick consecrated salt, and then killed before a crucifix. The priest, in eating his portion, consumes the sins of his congregation. Some Armenians apparently still believe that only a sacrifice after their deaths can atone for their sins. [*Later I learned that the then Catholicos of the Armenian Apostolic Church, Vazgen I, has tried with limited success, to do away with ritual sacrifice.*]

The Geckard monastery is unique, for its several churches are in continuity with a complex of rooms, including chapels and mausoleums, carved inside an adjacent rock outcropping. Within the rock, sculpted pillars and arches mimic those of a constructed church with interconnecting rooms. Most are lighted only by banks of votive candles in sandboxes, but one, a miniature chapel, is illuminated by shafts of light that enter through small windows open to the outside, part of an intricately sculpted dome.

On the lintel of an archway two chained lions face each other sculpted in the rock. Below them, a great eagle with outstretched wings holds a sheep dependent in its talons, the insignia of the Broshian dynasty. A prince of this family, Brosh Khaghpagian, built the complex between 1215 and 1230 A.D. His wife and son are buried here in a mausoleum carved in the rock.

Clearly an immense amount of work was required to hollow out the rock. Who did the work? Who took everything away, leaving a chapel and a mausoleum with arches, domes, and bas relief sculptures for us to wonder at centuries later? Who planned it, and how was it done? In my mind I pictured clinking tools and shadowy figures, scuttling back and forth in the gloom, morcellating rock and carrying it away. What sustained them? How much was faith, how much fear? How many worked here? How were they dressed? What were their tools? What did they eat? How long was their day? No answers, of course, but wonderment remains.

Below the monastery, a stone bridge crosses a rock-filled stream. Beyond, a path leads to a large cave, its walls and roof blackened with ancient soot. Along the way the trees have pieces of cloth tied around their branches, so many that they appear to be in bloom, similar to ones that we had seen at Lake Sevan. I asked Gagik what these rag flowers meant.

"This for girls to get married," he said. "They put cloth on trees in holy places and make prayer for husband."

Geckard is a sacred place for Armenians. Among those who found their way here today were several families, now picnicking in a grove above the monastery. Nearby, under a shelter, a galvanized iron counter had been used to prepare sheep after their sacrifice. Hordes of flys buzzed around flayed, inside out skin, and buckets of entrails. The air was smoky and redolent with the smell of meat cooking, a meal to be shared with the monks.

After leaving the monastery, we drove back to Guarni where we met the father and uncle of a little girl on whom we had carried out a burn reconstruction three weeks ago. We followed their car to a farm where relatives—brothers, wives and children—milled around the farmyard, preparing a cookout to honor us. After introductions, the men took us to a nearby shady grove where a long cloth-covered table stood in deep grass, under an enormous cherry tree. The men told us, through Gagik, that their great-grandfather had planted the tree eighty years before. It would be hard to imagine a more pleasant spot for a meal. Nonetheless, when I saw the table I cringed—vodka glasses stood beside each plate, and this after last night.

The men had killed a lamb just before we arrived and, as at Gekhard skin and intestines lay steaming on the ground. Nearby, a fire burned in a deep circular pit sunk in the earthen floor of an outbuilding. There was a smaller blind pit beside the larger one. To complete the cooking complex, a large pipe slanted from ground level, disappearing into the earth to emerge at the bottom of the firepit, the draft for the fire. I understood the fire pit and the draft, but I didn't understand what the blind pit was used for.

"For the legs," Gagik translated, "the women put their legs in the hole while they make lavash. She will show you."

Our little patient's aunt—she and her husband live on the farm— showed us how this traditional Armenian bread is made. She sat at a large low table, constructed like a butcher's block, and rolled out dough with a long rolling pin. Then she laid the paper-thin sheet of dough on a curved, ovoid appliance, covered with canvas with a hole in its back for inserting the hand. The implement looked, both in size and shape, like a shield. Was this how lavash was first made, by soldiers and camp followers baking it on shields as they sat before a campfire? The woman sat with her legs in the smaller pit and held the shield-like utensil over and partly within the large one, where the fire had now subsided to a glowing bed of coals. The dough cooked, almost in seconds, into a thin, flat, soft, lightly browned, sheet of lavash. As she demonstrated this, her husband threaded alternating thick slices of lamb and potato onto skewers which he laid over the pit to cook. Then he chased us away to have coffee while we waited.

As we sat at our table, several small boys came to visit us. One—he may have been ten—had a slingshot poking out of his shirt pocket. Here was something familiar from my own childhood. We found a suitable stone projectile. Thirty feet away a bucket hung from a tree. I took aim, compensated with twenty degrees of elevation, and let go. The rock struck the bucket with a resounding clang. Bull's-eye! Applause from the table. I surrendered the slingshot. I thought I saw a look of admiration on the boy's face.

Later, the men joined us, and the women brought starters of cheese, tomatoes, and cucumbers. Then came plates of roasted tomato, eggplant, and pepper cooked over the coals. Lavash and bread were heaped beside each plate. Now plates of barbecued lamb and potato arrived. Bottles of Boris Jelsen appeared and toast followed toast. We drank to ourselves, to them, to American doctors, to American nurses, to our families, to Armenia, to brotherhood, to women, to children, and to many other worthy things. I asked where the women and children were. Would they join us?

No, they ate separately. The women cooked, although the men cooked the meat. And so it went. We all talked to the Armenians through Gagik, and among ourselves as we got to know each other. It turned out that both Ingrid and Jayne have children in their twenties. Dan De La Pava gallantly opined that the nurses must have gone from the crib to a double bed.

The barbecued meat was followed by lamb that had been boiled in an enormous iron pot. Both the meat, and the broth in which it had been boiled, were delicious. Finally, the ladies brought bowls of yogurt, very plain, and very good, although the servings were much too large to finish. We went on to an emotional leave-taking "our house is yours for as long as you are in Armenia, whenever you want to use it," with heartfelt thanks on our part to these generous and gracious hosts. The weekend was a fine introduction to Armenia for our new recruits.

Monday, 23 August 1993

Five patients with malformed ears arrived this morning. That's a lot to show up all at once. Is this chance? Or is it because we are the only surgeons who treat ear anomalies here? Or because there is an actual increased incidence of ear malformations among Armenians? Armenia, so far as I can learn, does not gather data on birth defects that we might turn to for answers. There were also the usual patients with old burns, and children with poorly repaired and severely scarred cleft lips. All needed surgery. After seeing patients, we skin-grafted the soldier on whom we had done the muscle flaps last week, and then amputated another soldier's deformed and useless index finger. I called Barbara this evening. Everything is fine at home. At four dollars a minute, our calls are short. The electricity went out while we were talking. This occurs now every day. It usually comes back on in half an hour or so, but sometimes stays off for much longer.

Wednesday, 25 August, 1993

In spite of all the patients we see, we are not scheduling enough surgery. We did a popliteal z-plasty to release a burn scar in a child, and then placed a skin expander in a young woman's neck for the eventual release of a burn scar. Dan De La Pava leaves tonight; it was a pleasure to have had him here.

Thursday 26 August 1993

Today, the Armenian surgeons corrected more protruberant ears. They have operated on so many that they can do them as well as I can.

"No more ears on my time," I said."Do ears after I leave. For now, operating time is better spent on cases to which I can contribute something."

While we were in surgery a sixteen page killer fax came in from the the States. Directed mostly toward Mike McIntyre, it was filled with demands. Mike departs for the States in four days and evidently the AGBU is afraid that he will leave loose ends. The communication implied that he has been delinquent and had not submitted previously requested reports and information, including surgical statistics.

As Mike read the list aloud, he went to his files and one after another retrieved copies that he had previously submitted for all of data requested in the fax; he had sent everything in the past. The fax went on to complain about Abo's transportation costs, a substantial part of the Unit's monthly expenses. Considering the amount of running around that he has to do, the complaint doesn't seem justified. The organization has spent a couple of million dollars on the project. If we are into saving money, the first thing to do would be to stop the almost daily phone calls to and from New Jersey. At four dollars a minute, these must average two hundred dollars a day.

The fax ended with two interesting items:

"We are pleased to inform you," the first one read, "that we have had a productive visit with Dr. Hamlet Tamasian, the Director of the Surgical Institute. . . . He has agreed to transfer Dr. Garegin Babloyan to another service." This announcement met with approval, but the next one did not. The fax continued: "In an attempt to smooth over past frictions, the AGBU has agreed to allow the Director to oversee the PRSC. . . ." It is a decision that, if implemented, effectively makes him the Unit's manager. The Armenian doctors can't believe that the AGBU would take such a step. They have been sold down the river. They won't work under such an arrangement.

Today's final event was a meeting with the Director who has just returned from the States. Armine and Gagik came along to translate. We entered his first floor office through an airlock, protected on each side by two heavy wooden doors—a strange arrangement. What is he afraid of?. The walls of the office are covered with deep red fabric, and the room is filled with electronic equipment.

Tamasian is a middle-aged man, short, and darkcomplected. He never smiles. His eyelids are baggy and his teeth are gold-capped. His speech is more than staccato; he barks. Our meeting was cordial, and we discussed nothing important. He asked me if there was anything that I wanted to say. I told him that there are things that we need to talk about. We agreed to meet on Monday.

August is almost over. It has been a long and not particularly pleasant month. If I hadn't been so alone it would have been better. September will be better now that there are the American nurses to talk to and Cathy Vlastou will visit. The doctors have asked me to come back in April. I doubt that I will, but I'll consider it.

Sunday, 29 August 1993

Up at 7:00 a.m. after listening for a while to the BBC. The news is the same every day. The world changes in slow motion. Fighting in Bosnia, Israel and Palestine, Nicaragua, India, Pakistan. Last week a VOA announcer said that forty-eight wars were being fought around the world, so many that news services have trouble covering them. Here, the Armenians (oops, the Karabakhis) are fighting the Azeris. In Georgia, Eduard Schevardnadze's central government is fighting with ethnic minorities. The Abkhazis want to be Abkhazia, a state of their own.

On my evening walk I stopped at the store at the corner of Abovian and Sarian streets and bought a can of caviar (5000 rubles, about $4.50.), a lot of money in Armenia. The Russian writing says Osetra and Sevruga on the cans. Back in the apartment I ate the caviar on thin slices of buttered toast with cold vodka. I don't much like living alone—one must do as one can.

Monday, 30 September 1993

As this is our day to see new patients, we scheduled only two small cases. We divided the forehead flap to the rat-bitten child's nose, did a dressing on another child who had an extensive burn reconstruction last week, and then at 3:00 I met with the Director.

Tamasian was wearing the same red blazer with rolled up sleeves that he wore on Thursday, a white shirt with red striped pocket, and a loud tie. He scratched on a pad from time to time. He chain smoked and looked bored. He is surrounded with more electronic gadgets than I have ever seen in one office. On his desk there are two two-way radios, two fax machines, three telephones, a phone switching unit, an answering machine, and a computer with an Armenian program up on the monitor. I counted five other monitors in the office. One showed "Super Channel" which Armine tells me is a European equivalent of CNN. Reception was excellent; fortunately the sound was off. In the opposite corner another monitor displayed an operation in progress in the hospital's main OR. A smaller monitor scans the outer office. There are more electronic devices next to his desk, gadgets that I didn't recognize. They emit a continuous cacophony of buzzes, whistles and alarms. When a noise becomed too bothersome he touches the appropriate machine to cancel it. The office would be funny in a movie (cut to *Dr. Strangelove*), but here it is not.

We discussed problems. Garegin Babloyan was first. Tamasian says that he will not be transferred, after all. He will stay with the unit, but first he will take a ten day vacation to "get over his nervousness." The agreement that Tamasian made with the AGBU apparently has, as predicted, evaporated. Next, he agreed that there is a need for outpatient surgery, although it is a new concept for Armenia. He saw that same day surgery works in the United States and he plans to institute it here. I mentioned next that an average hospital stay of nineteen days is excessive. He agreed; inefficient bed utilization is an unfortunate holdover from the Soviet era. These and many other inefficiencies evolved over a long period and cannot be cured overnight. They will in time be corrected, certainly a reasonable answer.

Next, we discussed the need for another surgeon. The AGBU had also discussed this with him during his visit, and they mutually agreed that any surgeon newly appointed to the Unit must be chosen: first, with the approval of Gagik and of the AGBU; second, must have the equivalent of three years of general surgery; and third, must speak English. When I mentioned these requirements he barked—*he* will choose a new surgeon! Forget the AGBU's requirements! He lowered his voice then, and said that the surgeon that he appoints may be a better surgeon than Dr. Stamboltsian and if so, Gagik would have to live with it. What did that mean? Was he implying that Gagik has surgical shortcomings (in point of fact, he is an adequate, but unexceptional surgeon). So who does he have in mind?

Finally, I touched on the sensitive matter of past problems between the Unit's personnel and himself. I wrote in my notes that everyone must accommodate, if the Unit is to run smoothly. While an elitist attitude on the part of the Unit's American-trained personnel may have caused trouble (or so he complained in the States to the AGBU), his dictatorial actions have also contributed to the problem. Now Armine dug in her heels. She refused to translate. She said that she did not know what I meant, so she couldn't go on. Oh? Armine speaks English as well as I do. My willingness to speak out, in disregard of the consequences, frightened her. She was in effect saying "It's all right for you to speak thus to this man who likely was an honor graduate of the Joseph Stalin school of hospital administration. In a few weeks you'll fly away, but I'm here for life."

Tamasian saw that I was irked. He asked me for my notes so that he could have them translated into Armenian. What will the next translator do with the word "dictatorial?" At this juncture, after the usual pleasantries, our meeting ended.

Tuesday, 31 August 1993

A depressing day. The import of the meeting with "Omelet" (the Armenian pronounciation of "Hamlet") sunk in. Garegin will not be transferred, as promised, and there was no indication that the Director will work with Gagik or the AGBU at any level of cooperation. Next, Gagik summarily fired Abo, our driver. Abo, he says, costs too much. The instructions to do so came, Gagik said, from the States. Abo's dismissal was a surprise and disappointment to those of us who ride with him, for we like him. Later, Mike McIntyre—who leaves tomorrow—and I talked about my meeting with the Director. Mike smiled and asked if he had his operating room monitor on, the one that shows surgery in progress. Then he asked if he had used his two-way radio to give instructions to the surgeons of the operating team, as he often did.

"He has no idea how to use that computer." Mike said. "A lady comes in each morning and puts his schedule on the screen (that is what I had seen) and it stays on all day. That's all that the computer does."

I will miss Mike. He is knowledgeable about the Unit's problems on one hand, and about all that is going on in Yerevan on the other.

This morning I repaired an incisional hernia on an obese patient, one that had been operated on many times before. It was enormous, larger than the man's head, with several overlying deep ulcerations on the skin. I suspect that the original problem was a perforated appendix with wound infection, as the hernia protruded from a fairly small defect in the right lower quadrant of the abdomen. The dissection of the sac was tedious for the gut was adherent to the ulcers. Eventually we were able to isolate a well defined ring, much smaller than the size of the hernia suggested, but still much too large to close directly. We were prepared to use a flap from his thigh, but that seemed like overkill, given the size of the defect, and we ended up using plastic mesh. It closed the defect very nicely.

I pleaded with Karen Manvelyan, who is a competent anesthesiologist, for a smooth emergence from anesthesia, but the patient woke wild and straining. I knew that the repair was strong—we had used many heavy nylon sutures—but I was afraid that it would break down on the spot. Still, I couldn't feel any sutures pop, so it may be OK. Stormy emergence from anesthesia is not uncommon, particularly in smokers, nevertheless it is troublesome, especially when it occurs in a patient like this. If the repair survives his anesthetic emergence, and if it doesn't get infected, the patient should do well. [*He did. No infection, the hernia was cured, and he was happy. Just before I left Armenia he came to the hospital and gave me an enormous cut glass bottle of the finest cognac.*]

After we finished I found that Tamasian has struck again; he must have had my notes translated. Last evening, Ashot, the AGBU's office manager at the American University, refused to let our secretaries use the fax machine there (it's the only one available to us). He told the secretaries that every message must now be countersigned by Tamasian before it can be transmitted. This evening I stopped off at the American University and told Ashot, in language that I'm sure was more forceful than he is used to, to leave our secretaries alone. I anticipate no further trouble there.

Next, Tamasian has appointed a new "surgeon" for the Unit. It is a woman who speaks no English, and who has, so far as anyone can ascertain, never seen the inside of an operating room. He told Gagik this morning that it is up to us to teach her to be a plastic surgeon. It's worth noting—surgical inexperience aside—that the lady has irreproachable credentials: her mother is the head of the hospital's main ICU. Even better, her father is a top police official in Yerevan. Tamasian knows that she is not qualified, either as a surgeon or even as a trainee. I suspect that he doesn't want to tell her so for fear of upsetting her family. He wants us to do the dirty work. The appointment is, of course, unacceptable.

Thursday, 2 September 1993

Yesterday we operated on the little girl with the terrible burn of her lower face and chest. The heavy hypertrophic scar has contracted and pulled her chin down almost to her sternum so that her neck is fully and intractably flexed. I wanted to cut the scar under local anesthesia so that the anesthesiologists could extend her neck for their anesthetic intubation. They wanted to try to intubate her trachea blindly, without visualizing her larynx. I thought that could not be done, as her neck is too tightly flexed. We debated this back and forth. In the end, I felt that I can only advise these doctors—there are things that they must learn for themselves. I was correct, of course. The intubation attempt brought on severe laryngospasm and we had to cut the scar without any anesthesia. Karen could then extend her neck and pass the endotracheal tube. Gagik and Leon skin grafted the enormous defect. Their skin graft is too thin. It will contract, I suspect, and she'll need another procedure.

In spite of the initial anesthesia problems, the child did well. I feel frustrated when things like this happen. I have been there so often that I know what to do, and how to do it. Although it turned out all right in the end, it was a hair-raising ordeal for the doctors, and a terrible experience for the little girl. I feel like Cassandra: blessed with foreknowledge and fated not to be believed. I don't feel that I should insist that the staff do everything as I say. My role should be that of an advisor. Too, there are many ways to do things. Often there is no absolute "right way" or "wrong way" in surgery, only better and worse ways. Nonetheless, the case could have been a lot easier for the patient, for the surgeons, and for the anesthesiologists, had they listened to me.

Today, I debrided the flap that we put on the old man's face. The very end of it—the part that we needed most—died. There was a large hematoma (blood clot) under it. He will need a free flap. I will put that off until Cathy Vlastou arrives. While plastic surgical patients seldom die, their transferred tissue sometimes does. It is disturbing when it happens, for usually it means more surgery for the patient.

As I was waited in the OR between cases, I received a call asking me to go to the Director's office. He was entertaining a group of surgeons and wanted me to meet them. I went, but as always, there was no way to talk with them. The American nurses were there, too. Hamlet served wine and vodka and offered toast after toast. He announced plans (Gagik translated) to start a nursing school at the Surgical Institute. It will, he says, be as good as any American nursing school. An American nurse is coming to Armenia and she will help him with the project. The course will last for three months. Hamlet must believe that Armenians are very clever, or that Americans are very slow, for nursing schools in the States require three years. Still, it is a beginning; nurses are needed here.

I excused myself after a bit, as we were about to take a baby to the OR. A bilateral cleft lip repair done last week had separated. This occurs fairly often when both sides of wide bilateral clefts are repaired in one stage. We re-sutured it under local anesthesia and I think it will be OK.

Friday 3 September 1993

This morning I went with our doctors to the hospital's weekly surgical meeting. The auditorium is modern and comparable to ones found in good American hospitals. The conference makes use of an interesting teaching technique that I have not seen before. Three large TV monitors hang from the ceiling. Each department videotapes unusual or difficult cases. The department head describes indications, surgical technique, findings, and so on, and then the cases are discussed. Gagik presented two cases: the enormous hernia that I repaired, and the little girl with the neck contracture. Tamasian chaired the conference. He sat at a desk that stretches across the front of the stage and chain smoked during the entire meeting, the only person in the auditorium allowed to smoke. Attendance was excellent and almost every seat was filled.

"No one dares be absent." Armine whispered. I believe it.

From time to time, as the chiefs of the various departments presented their cases, Hamlet barked out remarks and occasionally shouted at the speakers. Once, he screamed at a surgeon who was presenting a case. I asked Armine why he was so upset.

"He didn't like it because some of the tape was fast-forwarded." Armine whispered. Again, toward the end of the session, Hamlet became irate and screamed at the audience.

"YOU MUST ASK QUESTIONS!" Armine translated.

The audience gratefully lit up as they left the auditorium. Tamasian's performance reminded me of the Russians depicted in our cold war spy movies.

Because of the meeting, surgery did not begin until after noon. Our first patient was a young man. Leon Torrosian, the young surgeon who joined the Unit just before I arrived, had operated on the man for microtia (a congenitally absent ear) before I arrived. The patient had lost the soft tissue over a cartilage graft and the cartilage is now exposed. The result wouldn't have been satisfactory, anyhow, as there is not enough definition of the reconstructed helix (rim of the ear.) There are so many microtic ears here that someone, Leon presumably, should learn how to do them well. I don't much like these cases, and never saw a really good reconstruction of a microtic ear during my years in Cleveland. I sent those who could afford the trip, to California where Dr. Burt Brent's results for this condition are excellent.

Our patient seems to be a spaced out kid. He had no available local skin to use for covering the exposed cartilage, so we used a skin grafted fascial flap from the scalp behind the ear. The flap had excellent circulation and bled profusely right down to the end. If this does not work, I will be most surprised. [*I was surprised. The flap was taken from below the skin of the scalp, leaving the overlying hair-bearing skin in place, and this was skin grafted. First the stitches pulled out, and then the flap came away from its bed. Eventually it died. I strongly suspect factitious—i.e., self-inflicted—manipulation on the patient's part. Surgeons occasionally encounter this in disturbed patients, although it is difficult to prove.*]

After we finished, I talked with Karen Manvelian about recruiting surgeons for the Unit. It came up because a maxillofacial surgeon presented an ear reconstruction in the conference this morning. I asked Karen why, because there is no maxillofacial service in the hospital, the surgeon did not join our Unit.

"He'd like very much to be on our service," Karen said, 'but he'd lose too much money. He'll get the equivalent of one hundred dollars just for the case that he showed, whereas if he was on our Unit, he'd only get one hundred dollars a month from the AGBU. Nobody who's any good is going to give up income to join us."

He went on to say that Armenian surgeons bill for their services, although it is illegal for them to do so.

"It's not just the surgeons who bill patients," he said, "all medical personnel do it. It's the Soviet system of 'tips.' It's the same everywhere in the former Soviet Union."

The AGBU forbids billing and instead gives the surgeons a monthly stipend, one which doesn't approach what they make on other services. Karen continued:

"Take Gagik. He'd make at least four hundred dollars a month, and probably more, if the AGBU permitted him to bill his patients. Armine and I would get at least twice as much as we're presently making. Only doctors who are making less money than the AGBU pays will come on the service. And that probably means that they're no good, because if they were any good they'd be making more money."

Another movie: it is an Armenian language version of *Catch-22*.

I had assumed that there was an exchange of money between patients and physicians, but was uncertain how the system worked. The bottom line is that surgeons who join the Unit are either—like Leon—early in their career and want to become plastic surgeons, or they are further along and have not been successful. The Unit's doctors, those whom the AGBU sent to America, are willing to give up income because they are loyal to the organization. For how long this will be so is a question that is yet to be answered, but I suspect in time financial reality will trump loyalty.

This complex system extends far beyond the physicians who provide direct patient care. Radiologists, pathologists, and all other specialists also receive their tips. Nurses receive rubles for every service; so also for laboratory personnel and others. As Karen and I talked, I realized what this pervasive tip system means for patients. Fees in the aggregate climb until they equal, or even exceed, what patients would pay for similar medical care in the West. I asked Karen whether I had it right.

"Exactly," he said, "it's how socialized medicine, Soviet style, works."

The health care system in Armenia is in transition and in time a legitimate fee-for-service pattern will probably evolve. For now, the present system, illegal and pervasive as it is, remains an example of how the Soviet economy functioned. Doctors, in general, do well under the system and some even prosper. Mike McIntyre had told me that Tamasian receives enormous kickbacks. Forty percent of every surgical fee collected goes to the hospital and a large portion—or so everyone assumes—is diverted into the Director's pocket. Mike was in Tamasian's office one day, and saw him take a roll of American hundred dollar bills out of his pocket and peel off three to give to someone. Mike believed that there could not have been less than $20,000 in the roll.

Sunday, 5 September 1993

The American personnel had been invited to attend a celebration today, honoring the founder of the Surgical Institute, Alexander Mikaelyan. He was a prominent cardiothoracic surgeon, known throughout the Soviet Union, who died two years ago.

We arrived dressed in our best clothes for it was a formal affair. The ceremony began at 2:00 p.m. with a procession. The surgeon's widow, a handsome woman, left the hospital's main door, preceded by eight nurses walking two abreast. Each carried a single, large, dark red chrysanthemum. The procession ended at a bronze bust of Mikaelyan in front of the hospital. The widow laid a bouquet of gladioli at the base of her husband's monument and then we adjourned to the auditorium for the remainder of the ceremony.

The auditorium was decorated with masses of flowers and overflowing with guests. The program consisted of slides and film clips showing Mikaelyan. He was not an old man when he died. In every slide and film clip he is smoking a cigarette. I suspect that he died either of heart disease or cancer of the lung. Canned music accompanied the whole show. Clearly, it took a lot of work to put together. Despite an amateurish aura, it came off well. The program closed with a long video clip showing Tamasian operating. This was followed by a shadow play. A back-lighted silhouette of a gowned figure, evidently a surgeon, appeared on a screen, its arm extended, as if giving a Nazi salute. Then Hamlet walked onto the stage, and faced the shadowed figure. We could now see that the figure was holding something in its outstretched arm. Hamlet went into the wings, and emerged holding a flaming basin on high. The silhouette represented Mikaelyan's ghost and the ghost had passed a torch on to our director. Hamlet held the flaming receptacle aloft for a few seconds and then put it down on the lectern. Now, to the sound of martial drumming, he descended from the stage and walked back and forth across the front of the auditorium flinging carnations to the audience. The drumming grew louder—dictator music—and the program ended. I have attended many ceremonies honoring men of medicine, but this was the strangest.

We filed into the lobby to find places at a long table covered with food: pastries, tomatoes and cucumbers, meats, and bread. Stands of bottles included Russian champagne, soft drinks, and, of course, vodka. The champagne was popular. Champagne is not my favorite beverage, but I tried it. It was potable, but too sweet, so I stuck to vodka as did most of the men.

As I was chatting with Ingrid, a short, plump, late middle-aged, and very determined woman forcibly and rudely shouldered her way between us. She was, she volunteered, the administrator of a large hospital in the States. She was clearly used to having her way and not at all concerned about what others might think. The woman abruptly asked what group I was with, a question which at first seemed odd, until I realized that no Westerners came to Armenia unless affiliated with an organization. I introduced myself and she told me her name. She is a Lebanese Armenian (many Armenians found their way to Lebanon during the diaspora) who had immigrated to the United States forty years ago. She came now to Armenia under the auspices of a benevolent organization, not the AGBU. She is the American nurse Tamasian mentioned earlier. She would help him inaugurate his nursing school. The woman was a good choice for she speaks Armenian.

After stoking up on food and vodka, Ingrid and I worked our way up to the head of the table to greet Hamlet's wife, Angela, whom I had not yet met.

"We have to do it," Ingrid said, "If we don't say 'hello' to her, we'll be fired."

She was referring to last winter's episode, when the Director fired all of the Unit's nurses because they had, he felt, slighted his wife. Angela and Hamlet were guests of the AGBU's medical coordinator on their recent trip to the States. The Coordinator said that Angela, unlike her husband, is a delightful person. Ingrid and Jayne had met her there when they visited the organization's office on their way to Armenia. They, too, found her to be a pleasant lady. She is an obstetrician and gynecologist and appears to be in her late forties. She and Ingrid chatted for a bit through an interpreter, and Ingrid made a date to visit her hospital. While they were chatting, I thanked Hamlet for inviting us to the celebration. As he listened to the interpreter, his eyes darted here and there about the room in the distinctive way that politicians have as they keep their eye out for the main chance, looking for situations and individuals that may benefit them.

Later, I talked for a few minutes with Gagik. Our conversation was similar to the one that I had had with Karen Manvelyan a few days earlier. We agreed that something must be done about the surgeons' salaries. Surgeons on other services get more for a single major operation than our doctors get from the AGBU each month. Gagik said that Armenia is undergoing a transition to a capitalist system. He believes that all of the Unit's patients should pay for the services that they receive. I asked him what he would do about those who had no money.

"Everybody has money." he said. "Maybe only a little, but everybody should pay, if only a symbol." I couldn't argue with that.

Gagik's cousin Artur, our new driver, was waiting for us outside. Artur turned up the day after Abo was fired, a circumstance that made us suspect that he had been waiting in the wings. We also wondered whether Abo's dismissal was influenced as much by Gagik's desire to provide a job for his unemployed relative as by the AGBU's drive to conserve funds.

Artur dropped me off at my apartment. The nurses had a date with the head of the Peace Corps in Armenia whom they had met on the plane. They are getting around, and learning much more about what is going on here than I am. I'm reminded of Plato's cave. I see shadows on the wall and try to infer from them what is happening in the outside world. Where do all the soldiers on the streets come from? Why are so many big, new, shiny Mercedes clustered around one building downtown? Why are there so many traffic police? Who gets the money that they extort from drivers? What is *really* happening in Karabakh? What is the political situation here? Who runs the country, politicians or the army? Is there a power elite? Has there been any recent change in Armenia's relationship with its neighbors? Has anyone interesting visited Armenia lately? I once read that an active interest in current events is a healthy sign in the aging. If so, I'm in good shape, but there's not much fulfilment to be had here.

Monday, 6 September 1993.

Today was quiet. Only a few patients arrived for us to evaluate. As it was clinic day, Gagik had not scheduled surgery. We all left early. I used the time to work on a status report requested by the AGBU's New Jersey office.

I wish that I knew more about how the Plastic and Reconstructive Surgery Center came into being. At the beginning, apparently, there was a glut of money that was spent with more enthusiasm than wisdom. Unfortunately no American surgeon came to Armenia during the early days of the project, someone who could have been involved with the Unit's construction and supervised equipment purchases, based on local needs and conditions. Most importantly, the situation at the Surgical Institute could have been assessed. It is not a good location for the PRSC.

I am unsure as to how much to include in a report. It does little good, other than for historical reasons, to list mistakes that were made when the Unit was organized. The future is something else. There will have to be changes, or the Plastic and Reconstructive Surgical Center isn't going to make it as a permanent resource for Armenia.

Wednesday, 8 September 1993

Today is the halfway point of my Armenian adventure. We hear that the President of the AGBU will arrive any day now. She is a lady whom Mike referred to as "the Empress of Armenia." I would like to go over the Unit's problems with her. A serious problem is that many appliances that were sent from the States are broken or have never functioned. I wondered, for example, why it takes so long to sterilize our instruments. I learned that two large sterilizers were sent from the States. Only one works, the other one never has, for it requires higher water pressure than Yerevan's water supply delivers. Evidently, nobody checked this out before the sterilizer was purchased, air-shipped to Armenia, and installed.

The Unit has a blood gas analyzer. It has never worked. There are six patient monitors. All but one are now kaput, victims of Yerevan's capricious electrical current fluctuations. Of two Carousel slide projectors, only one worked when it arrived, a requested part replacement has never arrived for the other. A new computer and laser printer came with the last flight. The computer only works intermittently. When a brown-out occurs, as often happens, the computer slowly, slowly gives up the ghost. Shades of HAL. Now I'm in the movie *2001* on the spaceship *Discovery*.

I've spent time with Mishak, the Unit's engineer, going over equipment problems. The sterilizer needs a pump to increase the water pressure. He asked to have one sent from the States, but was told to find it here, sort of like being told to find an ice-cube in hell. He showed me his correspondence file. It is full of back and forth faxes; ones that he has sent, and evasive or useless replies. Meanwhile, the walls of his office are lined with broken equipment. The truth is that sophisticated electronic equipment is unsuitable in this environment (much of it was unnecessary anyhow). High-tech medical appliances won't work reliably with Yerevan's erratic power supply, and even under optimal conditions, complex medical equipment needs frequent maintenance and service. There are, of course, no service facilities in Armenia.

A partial solution for the Unit's problems would be to shift its administration to Yerevan. I talked with the American nurses about this. We agreed that a manager, here in Yerevan would be best, preferably an honest Armenian. As I said "honest Armenian," we all laughed.

"Do you know what "honest Armenian is?" I asked

"Of course," Ingrid said, "It's an oxymoron."

To be fair, honesty is relative. We Americans should not judge the Armenians too harshly, for ethical standards vary within cultures, and America certainly has its share of graft and corruption. Everything here depends on favors. If I do something for you, you must do something for me. Western morality is different, evidenrly, than Armenian morality. A godfather ethic is not only tolerated here; it is the norm. Honesty, clearly, has different meanings in different environments.

Today, the Director called Gagik down to his sanctum to tell him that he will appoint a new surgeon, Artur Khocharian, to the Unit. He is presently with the Department of Microsurgery. Gagik and Leon have worked with him and like him He is a meticulous surgeon and he wants to be on our service. Artur speaks almost no English, but says that he will learn. I suspect that this man may be the surgeon that Tamasian mentioned earlier. The pendulum just may have swung in our direction.

After Gagik returned from his meeting with the Director, we went to see a patient on the Vascular Service. I was surprised by the difference between the two floors. Theirs is as shabby and bare as a prison hospital, whereas ours is well lighted and pleasant. Ours is not up to American hospital standards, but it's pretty close. Our rooms are so much better than those in the rest of the hospital that the other services board their VIP patients with us.

The patient that we came to see was a ten-year old child from Karabakh. She whimpered as a nurse carried her into the treatment room. Then, resigned, she lay quietly as her surgeon removed the dressing so we could inspect her wounds. She lost her right leg just below the knee Gagik said from a "bomb," but in his vocabulary anything that isn't a gunshot wound was caused by a "bomb." Her's was probably from a mortar round. for her back is peppered with shrapnel wounds of all sizes. She has a large, infected, tissue defect over her left hip. It needs to be cleaned up and skin grafted.

As I examined the child, the injustice of what happened to her took hold and I had trouble holding back tears. She is an innocent victim of man's compulsion to preserve ethnicity—tribal cohesion, group survival, "nationalism," whatever. It seems to be an imperative as innate as our drive to eat and to procreate. In the past, group loyalty surely had great survival value, but now it's a troublesome and dangerous atavism. Here, in Georgia, in Bosnia, in Ireland, in Sri Lanka, in Cambodia, throughout Africa, and elsewhere, children are suffering and dying.

Thursday, 9 September 1993

The Azeris are losing their taste for fighting, not surprising after nearly five years of war. The news reports that I pick up on short wave say that they are falling back. Karabakhi (and Armenian) forces are pushing forward and seem to be winning their struggle for Nagorno Karabakh. The Turks have responded by massing troops on the Armenian border and there has been shooting back and forth. Iranian troops are also gathering on the southern border.

The Armenians don't seem concerned. Gagik shrugs and says, "Is all political." What the news reports don't mention—and what the Armenians know—is that the Confederation of Independent States (CIS) remains under the cloak of Mother Russia. Russian soldiers guard the borders, so there is a certain ho-hum reaction here to the Turkish and Iranian posturing. Nevertheless, foreigners are concerned. The American nurses are aware of the foreign community's uneasiness and have taken the day off to go to the American Embassy to register. Turkey's parading of force is the nationalistic equivalent of a mass rally, a way of protesting what is happening to their cousins in Azerbaijan. The Armenians say that the Karabakh and Armenian forces could march all the way to the Caspian Sea and into Baku if they wanted to. Judging by the number of freshly wounded troops that we are seeing, fighting continues in Karabakh.

Today the orthopaedists were working on a soldier who arrived with a massive through-and-through gunshot wound of his mid-thigh. The field surgeons had debrided and splinted the leg and our surgeons will close the wound secondarily when it is appropriate to do so. Now they are reducing the splintered femur. Their method of fracture care is well suited to their limited equipment and lack of supplies. They use Ilizarov fixation, a technique I noted earlier. It originated in Russia and is beginning to be used in the States.

The surgeons place long pins transversely through the leg, inserting them like skewers, feeling for the bony shaft of the femur above and below the fracture site. When the pins impinge on the bone, they use a battery powered drill to pass them through the femur and on through the soft tissues on the opposite side of the thigh. Eventually, many pins transfix the leg. The pins are then fixed to circumferential rings that completely encircle the extremity. The rings, in turn, are linked from top to bottom by longitudinal rods to give a cylindrical, metal, cage-like exoskeleton.

The orthopaedists were using our operating suite because we have a "C-arm," a fluoroscope, used to check the position of the bone ends during the procedure. Usually they do not bother with x-ray control and make necessary adjustments to the bone subsequently, by rearranging the external hardware as needed. Their results are impressive. The Ilizarov technique is a clever and effective means of treating long-bone fractures, and variations of the same method are also useful for treating other orthopaedic conditions. Gagik says that there are eight hundred bed hospitals in Russia that treat patients, using this technique exclusively. I heard Ilizarov lecture when he visited the U.S. several years ago. He has since passed away. He practiced in Siberia and, lacking the equipment required for traditional methods of fracture care, devised his method out of necessity.

This morning I helped Leon repair two flexor tendons in no-man's-land. ("No-man's-land" refers to an area at the base of the fingers where flexor tendons pass through a narrow tunnel. Tendon repair here is difficult and results often leave much to be desired.) The case went well. I had misgivings about Leon at first, but I think that he will become a good surgeon. Later, I met with a recruit, Samvel, whose last name I didn't catch. He is yet another of the Director's surgical candidates. Samvel has no surgical background beyond a few months of emergency room work. I told him that he needs to get a foundation in general surgery before coming to us.

This evening, as I walked, I saw many more soldiers than usual on the streets. Maybe conditions in Karabakh have stabilized enough to allow them to be furloughed. I wonder how Armenia, which has nothing, can support an army. Armies in little countries start small and then, like rocks pushed from the tops of mountains, gain momentum. I have no way of guessing how much power the army wields in Armenia, but I suspect a fair amount. I do know, from caring for Armenian soldiers, and particularly from meeting the officers who come to visit the wounded, that these men are tough and very professional. I would not like to tangle with them.

Another long fax arrived today from New Jersey. The AGBU wants operative statistics for the last year: admission and discharge dates for every patient; length of hospital stay; the name of the surgeons and anesthesiologists for every case; type of anesthesia; where each patient lives; the source of each patient's referral to the Unit; information as to whether the case was clean, contaminated, or infected; and a description of any complication. Diagnostic code numbers are to be assigned to every patient and procedure. They also want similar information on every outpatient seen by a doctor. It is a hopeless request. Surgeon-patient encounters here are informal at best. They take place in the hall, office, and on other services' wards. While patients are encouraged to come on Mondays—and many do—others show up at any time, whenever they can find transportation. Because of the informality, and because of our surgeons' overall aversion to paperwork, it is realistically impossible to get an accurate listing for these encounters. There were more demands: for a directory listing the names and titles for all of the the Surgical Institute's administrative staff, their phone and fax numbers for hospital and home. Said directory should include the same information for all Yerevan and Gyoumri Hospitals and for other hospitals in other communities and for all service organizations that provide relief care in Armenia. Such correspondence is ludicrous and reveals a total detachment from the realities of the situation here. Worse, the never-ending string of ill-conceived communications upsets everyone.

Saturday, 11 September 1993

Last evening Ingrid and Jayne stopped by for a drink and afterward we went to Yerevan's only pizza parlor. The pizzas, made with rough flour, are small, but acceptable; the more so when one considers how much trouble it must be to procure ingredients. From there we trekked downtown to the Hotel Armenia on Republic Square. I had not been in the hotel before. The lobby is all marble and spacious, an Armenian version of the Ritz. There is also a cozy bar. Several therapists from the Red Cross Hospital sat at one table, and an American engineering consultant sat alone at another, so we all joined up.

I felt at home. American beer was a dollar a can and the barman accepted only American money and returned American change. Later, a small band played favorites: *The Girl from Ipanema, Summertime, Night and Day* and others. Ingrid and Jayne chatted with the therapists and I with the engineer. He knew all about equipment and communication problems in Armenia. He listened sympathetically as I told him about ours. He shook his head and said that he wished he had something to offer. Given circumstances here, there was nothing else he could say.

I worried about the nurses walking home on Yerevan's unlighted streets. They say that they are often out at night and are not even a little bit concerned, so I left them at the turn-off to their apartment. The long walk back to mine was uneventful. There were a few couples strolling; nobody seemed concerned. I thought how it would be to walk alone for several miles through a darkened American city. We also hear how dangerous Moscow is. For now, at least, Yerevan is safe.

Last week was busy. We did what the Unit was set up to do: cleft palate repairs, burn reconstructions, and other reconstructive cases. Gagik has decided, however, that he wants to do cosmetic surgery. (By way of definition: "cosmetic" or "aesthetic" surgery is defined as "surgery to improve the appearance of normal structures." It is lucrative for the surgeon and, strictly considered, is unnecessary for the patient. "Reconstructive surgery," on the other hand, corrects tissue abnormalities. They may be birth defects or the result of trauma or disease. Unfortunately, given the public's intense interest in cosmetic surgery, many believe that cosmetic surgery is all that plastic surgeons do. Some surgeons do specialize in cosmetic procedures, but overall it makes up only a small part, twenty percent, or so, of plastic and reconstructive surgical practice in the United States.)

Gagik's decision gives me some concern. If he occupies his time with cosmetic surgery, the Unit's primary mission of providing specialized reconstructive surgery will suffer. Nevertheless, I told him that I would help him do a breast uplift and a tummy-tuck. In capitulating, I rationalize that if cosmetic surgery is in the Unit's future, it would be best if he knows what he is about. It is not hard to get reasonable results with boobs and tummies, but I'm concerned about faces, noses especially. Armenia may be a mother lode for the procedure, but rhinoplasty, done well, is not a simple operation.

At mid-morning I walked downtown to the Hotel Ani. It is another landmark hotel in the busiest part of Yerevan. At some point in the recent past most of its rooms became business offices, so now it is more office building than hotel. I walked up three flights to the "Mafia Bank." Four men sit in a small hotel room. They smoke, they talk, and they wait. One is a doctor, a "reanimator," who worked with Armine. She says he is smart and a very good intensivist. He has an aura of quiet competence. As he made so little money as a physician in the Surgical Institute, he left to become a "banker." The word is a misnomer, for the Mafia Bank is simply a money changing operation.

I told the bankers that I wanted to change one hundred dollars into rubles. They examined my hundred dollar note with great care. I had been careful to bring all new bills with me, but this one had been in a sweaty money belt and was creased and stained. One of the men left the room and locked us in. He returned in five minutes, and handed the doctor a wad of bills. He divided them among the men in the room Finally, after much shuffling, the doctor gave me 140,000 rubles. Then, as I stood to go, he gave me several thousand more. I assumed that the first money was at the exchange rate, and the rest was a bonus for my business. Later, I learned that money changers will only accept new American bills of certain provenance because counterfeit money comes to Armenia from China, North Korea, or elsewhere. [*It was a mistake for me to change this much money. The value of the rubles remaining from the exchange were worth far less only two weeks later.*]

I walked to Republic Square from the Ani. Behind Lenin's pedestal I found a mall with a long pool. It contains 2750 little fountains. Constructed in 1982, it commemorates Yerevan's founding, supposedly that many years ago.* As with every fountain in the city, these and the pool itself are dry. Beyond the pool and its fountains, hundreds of men, and a few women, milled about, brandishing handfuls of money. Mike McIntyre told me that this is the location of what is the *de facto* Central Bank of Armenia. Because of continuous inflation, anyone who has rubles wants to trade them for foreign currency—dollars and reichsmarks—and they do so at this outdoor "bank," a mega-equivalent of the Mafia Bank in the Hotel Ani.

I walked next from Republic Square to the "Gastronom" on Abovian Street. The Gastronom was a state store and looks like the ones that we used to see in illustrated articles about the Soviet Union. Painted white metal and glass showcases line a large, white-tiled, central area. Most of the cases were empty. There was one section, however, where I saw bottles that just might be wine.

---

*The date of Yerevan's founding came from a cuneiform inscription uncovered on the site of an ancient Urartu fortress within the environs of today's city. The Urartus lived from the ninth to the sixth century BC, in the area around Mt. Ararat (the word "Ararat" is cognate with "Urartu"). The cuneiform tablets told how the Urartu leader, King Argishti I, built a fortress named Erebuni, on a hill that lies within today's Yerevan. The name "Yerevan," was derived from "Erebuni." The date that the fortress was built, 782 BC, is assumed to be date of the city's founding. While a definite date is convenient, it is necessarily arbitrary. Subsequent excavations have shown that settlements on this site antedated the fortress, possibly for millenia. In the sixth century B.C. local tribes, the ancestors of today's Armenians, infiltrated and overran the region, displacing the Urartu.

"Vino?" I asked.

"Da, vino!" I guess that "Vino," like "OK" and "no problem" is a universal term. Through sign language I bought four bottles, two red and two white, pointing to my white shirt for the latter. The wines were Armenian; the red from Guarni and the white from "Aracs" (Arax) in southern Armenia. At home, I tried the red wine with a late lunch; it was drinkable, but unimpressive. More impressive, however, is that the four bottles cost nine hundred rubles (64 cents), including a deposit for the bottles.

Sunday, 12 September 1993

I had a date this morning to meet the nurses at "Vernissage," the art market near Republic Square in downtown Yerevan. [*I had to look this up back in the States. "Vernissage" is an artists' term. It refers to the day before a show opens when paintings receive a final coat of varnish.*] Jayne had gone shopping on her own so Ingrid was alone when we met in Republic Square. I told her about the wine at the Gastronom so we went back there and loaded my rucksack with as many bottles as it would carry (nine, as it turned out) and then crossed Republic Square to Vernissage. Originally a market for arts and crafts, it has now grown to become an enormous flea market where Yerevanians shop, especially for hard to find items. We saw some surprisingly good oil, acrylic, and watercolor paintings, prints and craftwork. Old cameras fascinate me and when I saw a Zorki 35 mm. camera in the flea market I bought it. It is an exact copy of an early screw-mount Leica, with a collapsible, f3.5 "Industar" lens. I paid 12,000 rubles ($8.57) for it; at that price I couldn't bring myself to bargain. The new Nikon Lite-Touch camera that I brought with me quit on its second roll of film. I don't want to carry around the good Pentax SLR that I use for clinical photography and, since the Zorki is in like new condition. I'll see how it does as a walkabout camera .

We returned to the nurses apartment, killed a couple of bottles of Armenian "port" and looked at Marianne's snapshots. Jayne returned with carrots, potatoes and a chicken she had found in one of the big markets. She put together a chicken pot au feu and cooked it over a kerosene heater (as always, no electricity). It was delicious—a welcome change from big Ala's basic cuisine.

Monday, 13 September 1993

We saw patients in the morning and then went to the OR to operate on a severely deformed, burned hand. Three fingers needed to be straightened and the scarred and contracted palm needed a full thickness skin graft.

We'd planned to use a flap from the opposite arm, but I thought that a full thickness skin graft would be adequate. The man was totally hairy, so we used his upper inner arm for a skin graft donor site, as there was less hair there than anywhere else. It was best for this patient. (Skin grafts, especially thick ones as these were, retain their hair and other characteristics, when they are transferred from one site to antoher. Vampires are supposed to have hairy palms, but patients don't much care for them.)

Our day ended with a meeting devoted to the Unit's equipment problems. Karen Manvelyan wondered if the AGBU would purchase Russian anesthesia machines that could be serviced from Moscow. I wondered, in turn, how *that* would play in New Jersey. Karen's point is valid, however, for he is concerned about safety. The two anesthesia machines need parts and service, and soon he will have to cannibalize one to keep the other one going. I told him that I would discuss our problems with the AGBU. A solution might be to have a factory representative fly in from the States to service the equipment.

Then home for supper and a nap while listening to the radio. The Israelis and Palestinians were signing a peace agreement on the White House lawn and VOA was broadcasting the ceremony live. Then, per prearrangement, I talked with Dr. Vigen Darian in Detroit. He arrives as a volunteer in a few weeks. He has been on missions to South America and wonders whether Armenia is like Ecuador or Peru. Barbara and I have been on medical missions, both to Peru and Guatemala, and I could tell him that things are different here. Those countries—or parts of them, anyhow—are primitive. Armenia is not primitive, it is screwed-up modern. We talked for twenty minutes. He is double-boarded in both ENT and in plastic surgery and is interested in facial reconstruction. We have been putting cases aside that he may want to do.

Our first patient this morning was a Bulgarian TV journalist. She is an auburn haired, youngish (early to mid-30s), outgoing and attractive woman who has been covering the war in Karabakh for four years. She says that during that time snipers have shot two TV cameras off her shoulder. She didn't know whether her survival is a result of good luck, or good marksmanship. Then, several months ago, shrapnel took off the tip of her great toe. Gagik put a little skin graft over the open defect. The graft took, but the toenail impinges painfully on heaped up soft tissue at the end of the toe and she has trouble walking. I suggested shortening the phalanx and revising the nail. She is a tough, but pleasant lady, who fits my mental picture of a war photographer. I told her that the lidocaine block would hurt. "No problem." she said, and there wasn't.

I did the next case with Artur Kocharian, the surgeon whom Tamasian

View across Yerevan to Mt. Ararat (Macis). Mother Armenia silhouetted, right foreground

Mikaellan Institute, home of the Yerevan Plastic and Reconstructive Surgery Unit

Yerevan's Genocide Monument

Statuary at the Genocide Monument

Dusk in Yerevan; cranes looming above stalled building projects.

"Fill 'er up." Fuel tankers with gas from points unknown.

Gekhard Monastery

Figures sculpted in the living rock of the Geckhard chapel.

St. Mesrop Mashdots, inventor of the Armenian alphabet, in front of the
Matenadaran, Yerevan

Hand monument, downtown Yerevan.

Church of the Apostles on Sevan "Island." Girls seeking husbands knot cloth on shrubbery at all of the holy places in Armenia.

"Pagan temple" at Guarni

Making lavash. Rolled out dough is spread over the shield-like device. The "shield" is then held from inside, over the edge of the firepit.

Lavash is cooked in a few seconds when exposed to the intense heat of the coals.

Mother Armenia, on the heights above Yerevan.

Drs. Armine Kharatian
and Cathy Vlastou.

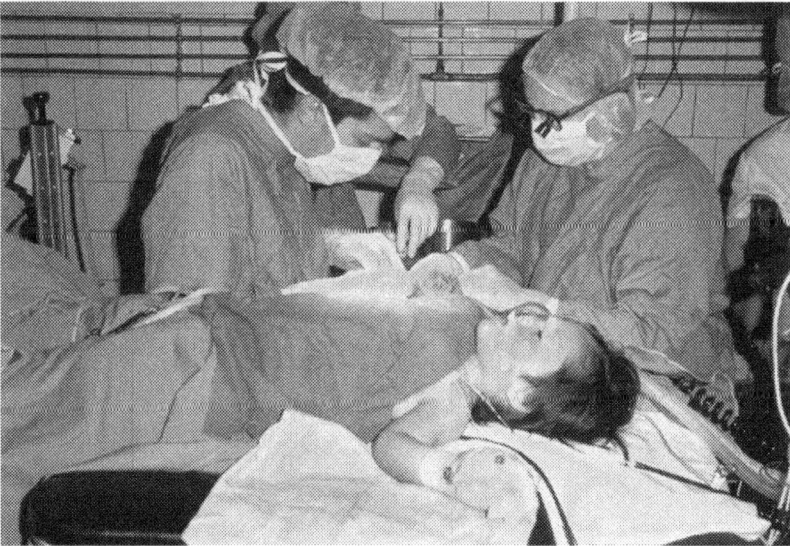

Drs. Cathy Vlastou operating, Karen Danielian assisting.

St. Hripsemeh's church, Mt. Ararat in the distance.

Sunday service, St. Hripsemeh's church.

Steps leading to Soviet-Armenian monument on the heights above central Yerevan.

Ruins of St. Gregory the Illuminator's church, the most ambitious of all of the ancient Armenian churches. It was built between 641 and 661 A.D. and destroyed by an earthquake three centuries later.

Ancient khachkar, or
cross-stone, com-
monly seen in holy
places throughout
Armenia

Yerevan Brandy Factory. Nurses Jayne Prentice and Ingrid Lusko.

The spear that pierced
Jesus' side,
Echmiadzin Church
Museum

Dr. Gagik Stamboltsian at the end of the day, relaxing with "Black Death"
vodka.

Khorvirap ("Dungeon") Monastery where St. Gregory the Illuminator was imprisoned. The Armenian-Turkish border lies just above and along the line to the right.

Cartridge cases and wildflowers on the Shushi battlefield in Karabakh.

Karabakh vista, from the battlefield at Shushi.

Lunch with the Karabakh KGB. The author on near left, Dr. Gagik
Stamboltsian near right.

Modern memorial khachkar, Stepanakert, Nagorno Karabakh.

Karabakh father-in-law monument.

has just transferred to our service. We replaced the skin on the back of a burned hand in a little boy. This is the child's second operation. A week ago, we released and grafted his severely scarred eyelids, so now he can close his eyes. Today's case also went well. Artur is an extremely competent surgeon—clearly the one Tamasian referred to earlier.

The nurses and sanitars ("sanitar" is a Russian term for ancillary OR personnel) don't understand why I use fine catgut stitches—as opposed to non-absorbable silk or nylon—to attach the skin grafts for our hand and burn reconstructions, particularly on children. I told them that it was so we wouldn't have to upset the kids—and the surgeons, nursing staff, and parents—during suture removal. The fine catgut sutures are quickly absorbed and don't have to be removed. The nurses then said that they didn't understand why surgeons preferred certain suture materials (something that I don't always understand myself) and asked if I would talk to them about it. This afternoon we met in the library and I lectured, sort of, for an hour. The qualification is because there was no way in which I could present an hour's worth of information; everything had to be translated. Short Nune had spent a year in Los Angeles with her grandmother, so she translated as best she could. The nurses and sanitars then volubly discussed each point among themselves.

I told them about the various kinds of suture material: natural fibers (silk and cotton), self-absorbing (catgut), and synthetic materials like nylon and polyglycolic acid. I spoke about the advantages, and disadvantages of each material and threw in a little history, explaining how, before the introduction of modern aseptic surgical technique, every wound became infected. Non-absorbable sutures, such as cotton or silk, acted as nidi for infection. Surgeons tried various types of leather sutures, because leather dissolved in the body. It turned out that catgut used for string instruments (derived not from cats but from sheep intestines) worked best. I told them how Sir Joseph Lister, then professor of surgery in Glasgow, Scotland, sterilized his catgut sutures with carbolic acid and used them in his operations. In 1867, he introduced antiseptic surgical technique to the world.

I think they understood, and they were obviously appreciative. I enjoy working with them. Communication in the OR is necessarily through the Armenian surgeons. They are not always present, however, and then matters get interesting. Nurses and sanitars scurry around, picking up one item after another, usually quite unrelated to what I want, and offer them to me. Still, the work gets done and most of our operations go smoothly. I am also, slowly, learning basic surgical Armenian and that takes care of the simpler needs. They show great glee when I try out my Armenian vocabulary.

Armenian language is strange to a westerner's ear, it has many consonants and few vowels. A few words are useful in the OR: *mkrawt* for scissors, *ktrel!* for cut!, *tel* for suture, *aserr* for needle, and so on. Some of the words are derived from Russian or English terms and that makes it easier: so *moskeet* for mosquito forceps (small hemostatic forceps), *pintcet* for forceps. Many of the Armenian words are compound, made up of sensible combinations. *Booj* means medicine, or treatment, and *cuir* means sister, so *boojcuir* is nurse. *Vira* is wound, so *virabooj* is surgeon. I see similarities to European languages, not surprising given their common Indo-European derivations. The verb "to be," for example, is conjugated *em, es, e, enk, ek, en* in the present tense; other verb endings are similar.

While I was waiting for Nune to unlock the library for my talk, I saw a little boy standing in the hall with his grandmother. Our younger patients usually have relatives in constant attendance, quite often grandparents. Relatives provide both meals and nursing. Their presence is often a blessing as our patients may receive no close attention otherwise, after leaving the ICU. I examined the child while I waited. He had severe burn contractures of his left axilla (armpit) and of his antecubital area (the space in front of the elbow.) These should respond well to release of the scars and z-plasties. When Nune arrived to translate, I asked his grandmother how he was burned. Five years ago in Karabakh, she told us, Azeris invaded their village. Soldiers burst into their home, killed her husband, and then took a pan of boiling water from the stove and poured it on the infant. The child had surgery of sorts in Karabakh. He has a long, wide scar running the full length of the front of his left thigh, the donor site for a thin strip of full thickness skin that a surgeon placed crosswise in the axillary contracture. It was worse than useless surgery. When I see patients like this, I realize that we really are filling a need.

After a long day, I headed to bed at 10:30. I didn't make it. I received a call from New Jersey. The conversation, after a few pleasantries, went sour. I had upset people there by mentioning the Unit's equipment problems in the report that I had submitted, and that they had requested).

"Mistakes made in planning this project are over and done with. Why are you bringing all these problems up now?"

I tried to explain that if the equipment isn't repaired we won't be able to operate. Apparently no one was listening at the other end. I was reproached for my "negative and complaining report."

"You don't realize how much work went into the Unit, how many consultants we had, and now you come on the scene and complain."

I do realize, of course; further, my composure was slipping as I tried to get in a few words.

"The first thing that I was told," I said, "was that the Unit had problems. I was asked to come to Armenia to identify them, and to make suggestions for solving them. I found problems. I told you about them. Now, *please*, listen. We can not operate if the equipment doesn't work!"

I paused, took a deep breath, then went on to say that I would suggest solutions for the various problems. The voice at the other end calmed down, and went on to tell me about Tamasian. He has, I was told, connections that go even beyond the country's president. He is believed to be involved in racketeering. Others are also involved, and all are at such a high level that no one can touch them. It is hard for me to believe that any hospital director, anywhere, can have that much influence.

As we talked, I remembered that Mike McIntyre had told me about a scam that involved Tamasian and a biologic products company in California. The plan was to use Armenians for blood donors. Blood products would be extracted and shipped to the States. Mike said that there were rumors of kickbacks and graft. I discounted his story; it seemed so unlikely. Then, today, Marianne spoke of an incident that had occurred while she was lecturing to medical students. The Director brought visitors into the room, interrupted her lecture, and had each of the students donate a unit of blood on the spot—for what purpose she did not know. My cinematic scenario has shifted again. Now, I'm in *Coma*; welcome to the Jefferson Institute.

I hoped that the conversation with New Jersey was finished; it was not. There were noises on the line.

"There are always noises on the line," I said, "so what?"

"It means that your phone is bugged. Our conversation is being recorded. It's time to hang up."

I agreed. I wasn't worried about a bug, but we had talked for more than an hour. I wanted to go to bed, but New Jersey was daytime fresh (Armenian time is nine hours earlier than U.S. eastern daylight saving time) and was not ready to hang up. I was asked about Tamasian's nursing school project. I relayed what little I knew. Apparently New Jersey believes that the nursing school project is part of a mixed-up skein of intrigue that involved competing relief organizations all of which resented the AGBU.

"Why so?" I asked.

"Because," I was told, "ours is the only modern surgical facility in all of Armenia."

Not true. The Surgical Institute's Cardiovascular Service is a modern unit, supported by another service organization. It opened last winter, when the PRSC opened. They have done about one hundred and fifty coronary bypass operations since then. The AGBU apparently knew nothing about this.

"How," I was asked, "do they maintain their anesthesia machines and other equipment?"

"They're having trouble, too." I replied "They don't know how they'll get their equipment serviced."

"How in the world could arrangements for service be made," was the response. "Armenia is so isolated."

Now we were going round and round in circles; that is what I had written.

"That's just what I wrote in my report." I answered. "But unless we get our anesthesia machines and other equipment repaired, we're going to be out of business."

The conversation continued, covering the same ground. I was exhausted. Clearly getting the PRSC funded and off the ground has been a truly major undertaking and the organization has pulled it off. Nonetheless, these calls disturb and depress whoever is on the receiving end.

Wednesday, 15 September 1993

The OR is a sanctuary. It has always been a place where problems, transiently at least, slip out of sight. And so it was this morning. I helped Leon close a cleft palate, and then helped Garegin with a bilateral cleft lip. Both cases went smoothly. It's unfortunate that Garegin has such a difficult personality, he could do much for the Unit. As it is, however, he is too disruptive to remain. I asked Armine if he had apologized to her for his abusive behaviour. He has not.

We finished early. We could have done more, but as we are keeping up with the flow there is little point in pushing. Catherine Vlastou arrives from Athens tomorrow. The Armenians ask me, what will she think of Yerevan? I expect that she'll think of it as other Westerners do; a run-down city that shows signs of a decent past. Yerevan is like a comely woman who suffers chronic illness bravely, while wasting away.

Last night, just as we were leaving the office, a fifteen page fax arrived. It was a new list of demands for trivial, non-essential information and busy-work that the New Jersey office wants the doctors, nurses, and secretaries to gather, or to carry out—work that is impossible for our busy staff to do. All hands have by now passed beyond resentment to a state of resigned annoyance. The solution is simple; unreasonable demands will be ignored.

Friday, 17 September 1993

Catherine Vlastou arrived this morning from Athens via Paris. Her flight left Paris at 9:15 p.m. and arrived in Yerevan on schedule at 2:15 a.m. An Aeroflot plane has *never* before arrived on time. As we hadn't expected her then, she waited at the airport for five hours. Understandably, she was thoroughly peeved. Is this the new Aeroflot? Probably not. A better explanation for the plane's promptness is that Vazgen I, the Catholicos (papal equivalent) of the Armenian Apostolic Church, and Armenia's most prominent personage, was on the flight.

After she freshened up, we ate breakfast, and then went to the hospital. The doctors were at their Friday meeting, so I showed her around the Unit, the ORs and the ICU. After the doctors returned we made rounds and saw outpatients. There are four free flaps to be done, and several other complex cases. We'll be busy during her stay.

The Director knew she was coming and asked to meet her, so this afternoon we swung by his office.

"I can't believe it!" she said afterward. "He's stepped out of a movie!"

She saw a strong-armed cold war Russian dictator. He sure fit that description today. He waved a long, banner-like fax that had just come in from the AGBU office. It described a shipment of supplies en route to the hospital, and included detailed instructions on what to do with them. He brandished the uncut fax while Armine translated.

"They don't have any medical knowledge," he barked, referring to the AGBU's New Jersey office. "If there had been a surgeon on the other end he would have just said 'I'm sending you sutures and supplies,' instead of pages and pages of this nonsense."

He was also provoked because I had reported the Unit's problems. Evidently everything I had said had been relayed back to him. Now I'm provoked, too. Henceforth, I'll try to settle matters here and forget long distance micro-management. The Chief of the Institute's Cardio-Thoracic service is an American trained Armenian. He is supported by another relief organization that allows him to administer his unit completely from this end. When I mentioned this to Armine, she said that was true, but he doesn't have the answers either, because he is also having problems with the Director and plans to move the Cardio-thoracic unit to another hospital. That seems, at this point, to be the only reasonable solution for the PRSC, as well.

This evening we went to Leon Torossian's apartment to celebrate his thirty-first birthday. We ate salads, vegetables, a wheat dish, and lamb, washing it down with Kool-Aid (big in Armenia), "wodka," cognac, Armenian champagne, and beer. The champagne was far better than the sweet Russian champagne we had last weekend at the hospital. The Armenian beer, the first I've had, was surprisingly good; light, with a pronounced wheat flavor.

As always, there were endless toasts spaced out over the evening, and everyone had a great time. Kids ran around and crawled under the long table. Cousins, mothers, neighbors, and friends came and went. An ancient grandmother with gold teeth was knocking back cognac. Supposedly one out of four Armenians lives to celebrate the Big One and this lady was well on the way. Americans believe that the Armenian diet explains their longevity. That may be, for it is high in healthy food: vegetables, greens, fruit, and yogurt. Average life expectancy will decline in the future, however, because almost all Armenian men and many of the women are heavy smokers.

Saturday, 25 September 1993

This morning Catherine and I trekked down to Republic Square to visit Vernissage and bought several prints of Armenian churches from a friendly artist. Next, we went to the Archaeologic Museum on Republic Square. Catherine was delighted to see and translate the Greek writing on the copy of the Guarni mosaic. Later, a cadaverous doorman at the Hotel Armenia told us about a bar that I hadn't heard about, hidden deep in the basement of the hotel. It was dark, cool, and empty, a perfect place for a lunch of cold-cuts, bread and beer. And then the long walk uphill to the apartment. I waved at Big Ala who was sitting on her sixth floor balcony, and when we arrived she was waiting with dinner.

Sunday, 19 September 1993

This weekend is a long and important holiday honoring the Republic of Armenia's third year of independence. I slept late, then went across the street to the market and bought fresh herbs: basil, parsley, coriander (identical to our cilantro,) and fresh oregano. This noon, Cathy made a salad of ripe tomatoes, onions, Kalamata olives and oil that she brought from Greece. We ate it with bread and a bottle of white wine—the bottle held 500 ml., just the right size for two people. Why don't they bottle it like that in America?

This afternoon, we walked around Yerevan. Many of its monuments are truly impressive. Among them is a memorial to Alexander Tamanian, the architect who planned the modern city. His massive stone figure, robed and reflective, leans over a drawing table on which he supports himself with outsized arms and hands. Behind him, an enormous set of doubled white marble steps rise skyward, gaining perhaps five hundred feet of elevation, to reach the city's heights. Four levels of indented alcoves are situated between the parallel stairs. Each alcove is uniquely sculptured and each has a variant pool and fountain (no water now, of course). The effect, if the memorial is ever completed, will be that of a great cascade. It is all abandoned now, and grass grows in the cracks of the steps. We plodded upward in the heat, meeting only an occasional couple descending. The steps peter out at the top. Here things are as they were when unpaid workmen walked away three years ago, leaving abandoned and rusting equipment, their project unfinished. There is only a dirt path at the top.

Another monument loomed above us, where the steps would have ended had they been completed. A great terrace serves as the base for a tall obelisk commemorating the first fifty years (of a total of sixty three) during which Armenia was a part of the Soviet Union. We climbed rickety wooden stairs to the terrace. All of Yerevan was spread out below us, tilting gently down to the Razdan River. Akhtanak (Victory) Park, another of the city's landmarks, is nearby. The park is large, densely wooded and has a small lake, now dotted with rowboats. The walks were filled with holiday people, and couples lounged on the benches lining the shaded walkways.

Yerevan's most impressive monument, the enormous figure of "Mother Armenia" stands nearby. She is a stern and martial woman, built like a lady weightlifter. She stands erect and vigilant on a high, multitiered, red stone pedestal. Her beefy right arm holds a partially sheathed sword. A seven-pointed star studded shield lies at her feet.

Mother Armenia, it seems to me, is the quintessential Soviet monument. She is, like many other monuments, large and impressive, but not particularly pleasing. Nevertheless she must be an improvement over the statue of a standing Stalin that previously occupied the pedestal. Armine told us that it was the last monument built to honor Stalin, and the largest in the USSR. After Khrushchev and the Soviet party congress exorcised the man of steel from the Soviet pantheon in 1956, all of his monuments disappeared. Something had to be done with all that bronze, so Stalin was recycled and Mother Armenia rose, like a phoenix, atop his pedestal. I suspect that the Colossus of Rhodes was about Mother's size. The Colossus fell, the victim of a natural cataclysm—an earthquake—rather than a social one. Evidently the Rhodians accepted the event as a divine warning, for the Colossus's bronze remains were carted away. I wondered whether anyone considered doing the same for the fallen dictator's remains.

As we wandered through the park we heard the sound of holiday music and caught occasional glimpses of an amusement complex where children rode dodgems, a carousel, a miniature railway, and a small roller coaster. Here, too, a great Ferris wheel stands. I can see it on the skyline above my apartment, although I had never seen it turning before. We stood looking up at it. An attendant motioned us over and insisted that we take a ride. He refused our money, saying only "Guests, guests." Up we went until we were even with Mother's head and could share her view as she looks out over her city to Ararat, the mountain known to Armenians as "Macis." It was dusk as we started the long walk down to the apartment. Lights were coming on everywhere, all over Yerevan, all at the same time, something that I had never seen before—electricity is usually rationed, block by block, here and there. Armenia needs more holidays.

Monday, 20 September 1994

Today is the anniversary of Armenia's third year of independence, so the hospital is essentially shut down. The AGBU's President invited all of the Unit's personnel to a celebration at the Opera House. Gagik picked us up early in the evening and led us to a reserved loge. Below us, the hall was overflowing. Banners in two languages on the stage's backdrop recognized the AGBU as the Yerevan Symphony's sponsor. The orchestra played a pops program. Although a few pieces were familiar, others were Armenian and the audience sang along. Between numbers, poets declaimed and the orchestra's conductor and other notables gave speeches. An attractive woman rose from her seat and danced in the aisle . Others joined in and soon the aisles were full of people dancing with their arms up and outstretched, which is how Armenians dance.

While this is a fitting occasion for celebration, I thought of what had happened to the country earlier in this century after the first world war, when Armenia was an independent nation for two and a half years. Then, thanks to an ill-advised military foray against Turkey, Armenians almost became, like the Kurds, a people without a country. I hope that Armenia's involvement in Karabakh, at the dawn of its new independence, turns out better. This little nation is not yet out of the woods.

Tuesday, 21 September 1993

Back to work. We did a latissimus free flap on the old man with the facial cancer. The surgery went very smoothly. It is a pleasure for me to work with Catherine again and the Armenian surgeons were impressed with a microsurgical case that went as smoothly as this one did. I hope that this will allow the patient to leave the hospital before his cancer recurs. He should have radiation therapy, but it seems not to be available here.

Thursday, 23 September 1993

We continue to be busy and are using both ORs. The Armenian surgeons are in the smaller one and Cathy and I work in the larger room. Today we reconstructed a difficult ear on a sixteen year old girl, the daughter of one of Tamasian's friends. The upper part of the ear was severely cupped and contracted. We were able to reconstitute the cartilage quite well, but then had to use a flap from behind the ear to fill the soft tissue deficit. It is not perfect, reconstructed ears seldom are, but it is an improvement.

Friday, 24 September 1993

Today I did a secondary repair of a cleft lip on an attractive adolescent girl while Cathy worked to reconstruct a burned leg and both feet on a child. Nothing could be seen of the toes; they were completely grown together, hidden in scar tissue, and the knee was severely contracted. She tried to release the knee with a Z-plasty, but there wasn't enough tissue so she had to skin graft the posterior calf. At that, she was unable to completely release the joint. The contracture has been present for so long that it is no longer a soft tissue problem. She brought the toes out from where they were hidden and skin grafted them. They should be nearly normal, but she was upset about the knee and felt that the case had not gone well, although I don't know what else she could have done.

Saturday, 25 September 1993

Even though it is Saturday, time is short so we decided to go ahead with a case that needs two teams working simultaneously. The patient is an older infant with multiple congenital abnormalities of her hands. Her mother had extra fingers (a condition known as "polydactyly") removed at some point, but the mother's deformity was mild compared with our patient. Three other siblings were also born with extra digits and her mother is pregnant again. Our little patient's deformities are much worse than those of her brother and sisters. She has ten fingers on each hand, including two complete, although angulated, thumbs. She also has compound syndactyly of the middle digits. ("syndactyly" is a condition in which the fingers are joined together for part or all of their length). Polydactyly is the most common congenital abnormality of the hands, but even so I have never seen as many supernumerary digits as this child has.

Our reconstructions were extensive. We worked on both hands simultaneously, removing the extra digits, straightening and stabilizing the remaining thumbs with pin fixation, and skin grafting the open areas where we separated the fingers. Fortunately, we had enough skin, using grafts from the discarded extra fingers. We were pleased with the result and I believe that her hands will function normally after they are healed. [*Nurse Jayne Prentice gave me a followup four months later. She told me, after she returned to the States, that the child's hands had turned out well.*]

Sunday, 27th September 1993

Today we went with the American nurses and an Armenian friend, Tigran, to Echmiadzin, northwest of Yerevan. It is the seat of the Armenian Apostolic Church and the site of a cathedral built at the time of the founding of the church in 303 A.D. Tigran works for the Armenian equivalent of the Internal Revenue Service. His car is a clapped out old Volga which he drives like an idiot. I wished that I had an ejection seat. Otherwise it was a fascinating day. We stopped first at an ancient church outside of Echmiadzin dedicated to St. Hripsemeh, a Christian martyr. The church is on a slight rise, with Mt. Ararat on the horizon to the west.

Sunday service was in progress. It was a striking pageant, enriched by the clergy's colorful robes and by a choir of two women and a man. The women's voices were beautiful, soaring and falling as they sang the long liturgy. The church smelled of beeswax from candles burning in sand trays, and it was lighted by shafts of bright sunlight, angling down and diffused by the candle smoke. The congregation stood, for there were no seats. The secularization of our services, it seems to me, has weakened religion by taking away its compelling mystery. We felt mystery in this ancient building. Armenians tell us that their church grows strong: they have no shortage of priests. Compare this with Catholicism's attenuation. There are, of course, other reasons for the decline of the Roman church, but I felt that the worshippers took strength from the ancient ritual that we saw and heard here.

St. Hripsemeh's church was built in 618 A.D. It is attractively proportioned, topped with the drum and polygonal dome typical of Armenian churches. Nearby ruins attest to the age of the site, but the church is fully preserved. After the service, we descended stone stairs to the saint's crypt. The saintly remains lie in a small stone casket decorated with an icon-like portrait. A woman stood at the side of the crypt singing an endless dirge as visitors came and went, crossing themselves and praying before a small shrine set into the wall.*

After we left the church we pushed the car to get it started. Its battery won't hold a charge and there are no new batteries in Armenia, at least at a price that Tigran can afford. We drove to nearby Holy Echmiadzin, the historic seat of the Armenian Church. The church's history is rich in tradition, much of which is centered on Echmiadzin and its cathedral. The cathedral is impressive, although far smaller and less ornate than the magnificent western European cathedrals—hardly surprising, as it was built many centuries earlier. Nevertheless, it has grace, simplicity and dignity, and is worthy of its place as the mother church of the Armenian religion. It, like every substantial building in Armenia, is built of volcanic tufa. Its dome is the same polygonal stone cone that I had seen at Sevan, Gekhard and this morning on St. Hripsemeh's church.

The service was nearing the end. It was sung by a choir, far larger than the one we had heard at St. Hripsemeh's. We stood in the entry as Vazgen I, the Catholicos, left the church. He is a bearded, handsome, man who, at 85, is a bit unsteady. Senior clergy walked at his side to provide gentle support.† A tall, thin woman, dressed in a fashionable white suit walked with churchmen and lay persons in the Catholicos's train. From what I have heard about her, I suspect that she is the President of the AGBU.

Later we visited an attached museum which contains many of the church's treasures. One of these is the spear, formerly at Gekhard monastery, said to have pierced Christ's side. It didn't look much like an operative spear to me, one that a Roman centurion might carry; it's too large and too ornate. Cathy asked me if I thought that it was the actual spear. I said that I thought that it *could* be, but if she were to ask me whether I thought that it *was*, I would have to say "no." We also saw a piece of the true cross (a very small piece), and several forearm and hand-shaped silver reliquaries, with their tubular fingers held in the age-old blessing posture, with thumb tip touching the ring-finger tip. These

---

*See appendix A for a history of the early Armenian church and its martyrs.

†Vazgen I died on 18 August 1994. He was born in Bucharest, served first as Bishop and Prelate of the Church's Romanian diocese, and then became Supreme Patriarch of all Armenians in 1955. He was a consummate diplomat who was able to maintain the church's integrity despite the USSR's official atheistic and anti-religious stance. The Armenian church's present strength reflects his superior leadership. From the obituary section, *The New York Times*, 19 August 1994.

contain bones of various saints, including those of Saint Andrew. We were obviously interested, so a young seminarian showed us around the museum and then led us down into a newly excavated cellar where we saw an intact pagan altar, discovered during recent renovations. The altar lies exactly below that of the cathedral above. Several crosses were neatly carved into the church's stone foundation. The seminarian told us that St. Gregory the Illuminator, the founder of the Armenian church, had carved the crosses, although he was unable to tell us how the attribution came to be.

We returned to Yerevan. On our way back, the ubiquitous traffic police stopped our car and fined us 15,000 rubles on the spot. Tigran's license plate had a chip. Ingrid made her indignation quite apparent, probably contributing to the size of the fine. We all pitched in to pay it. A miserable business. Terms like "highway robbery" and "police state" again came to mind.

Tuesday, 28 October 1993

Yesterday we did a free flap on a young woman with Romberg's hemifacial atrophy filling the defect with a muscle taken from her chest wall. We did a similar procedure today for the same condition in a young man, and a third one is scheduled for tomorrow. (In this condition, all of the soft tissues on one side of the face melt away from an unknown cause, leaving only skin and a thin layer of muscle over the underlying bone. The condition results in a grotesque, skeletal appearance on the involved side.)

The AGBU's President visited the Unit yesterday; it was she whom I had seen at Echmiadzin. She stayed only long enough to say, "Hello." Today, I met her. We talked about the Unit's problems. She seems to be, as I had been told, a practical, no-nonsense, business-like and intelligent woman. She is well aware of the Unit's difficulties. She asked me why the AGBU's American advisors had suggested purchasing so much inappropriate equipment. I stonewalled without volunteering that I suspected that it was because so much money was available, on one hand, coupled with little knowledge or appreciation of local conditions on the other. I did emphasize, however, that some of the broken equipment was badly needed for patient care. She said that she will arrange for its repair or replacement. The rest, that which cannot be repaired, or that we do not need, may be given away, or discarded. We spoke about other problems, including that of surgeon recruitment. She knows about the system of "tips," the basis of medical practice here. I mentioned that the difference in income between our physicians and those who work under the tip system prevents the Unit from recruiting good surgeons. Sensibly, she said that from now on the AGBU will permit our surgeons to go to a fee-for-service arrangement.

We talked then about the Surgical Institute's Director. She knows that it is impossible to work with him, but was unwilling to speak further about it, saying only that she had met with the Minister of Health and had been unable to get anywhere. Therefore, she said, the AGBU is considering moving the Unit to another facility. She believes, as I do, that a move may be the best solution, even though it will temporarily disrupt the Unit's function. Finally, somehow, she has managed to resolve the question of Garegin's status. He will be transferred to another department.

The President of the AGBU is the daughter of a wealthy Armenian-American industrialist, the inventor of a commonly used plumbing gadget. Clearly, she is a capable executive. Now, having had an opportunity to air my concerns, I'll stop worrying about the Unit's problems, many of which she seems to have solved anyhow.

Thursday, 30 September 1993

We were going to do our last free flap today, but the Armenian surgeons found an excuse to cancel the case. I wasn't upset. I don't handle long surgical cases and a heavy work load as well as I used to, and I'm running out of gas. I did a microsurgical anastomosis during yesterday's surgery, and announced that it was the last one that I would ever do. Catherine said not to make such grand and final statements, but I meant it and have no problem with it. Cathy wasn't unhappy, either, that today's case was cancelled, for it gave her a day off. We cruised around Yerevan (two more museums, gift shopping for things for her to take home: caviar, bastromah, etc.

She is a superb surgical technician and the Armenians are all impressed with her clinical knowledge, common sense, and meticulous surgical technique. Karen Manvelyan says over and over that she is the best surgeon that he has ever seen.

We took Cathy and Marianne Hess to the airport tonight (at 2:30 a.m.!) and saw them off. Marianne has been here for a year and was in tears. She has, she says, become an Armenian-American. It has been a great experience for her. They left from a new, modern airport that opened only a few days ago, and their departure went smoothly.

Friday, 1 October 1993

I helped Leon Torossian with a bilateral cleft lip. He did a good job and I was pleased with the repair. After that we reconstructed a severely burned hand on a middle aged man. His burn was similar to many others that we have seen, sustained when he used gasoline to start a fire during the cold of last winter. We had to release all of the web spaces, cover the exposed middle joint of the ring finger and amputate a useless, infected, little finger. Then we removed all of the thick scar tissue on the back of the hand, and covered everything with a thick split thickness graft from his thigh. It was a long procedure; tailoring the skin graft into such a large defect is like making a glove. As is typical with burns which have received inadequate treatment, the patient has lost motion in all of the small joints. He will have to work hard to get it back.

Saturday, 2 October 1993

The weather has been cool, with rain yesterday. The sun is getting lower. It doesn't reach the front of our building until late afternoon, so the apartment stays cool and gloomy for much of the day. Both Jayne and I have had diarrhea and fever for five days. A nurse who preceded us returned to the States with giardiasis. (*Giardia lamblia* is a common and troublesome water-born intestinal parasite.) Our symptoms are consistent with this, but who's to know? Yesterday, we both started on Flagyl, the drug of choice for giardiasis. Last night I woke with chills, cough, malaise, runny nose and eyes, and a headache, probably a flu syndrome of some type, unrelated to the intestinal problem. Cathy had it last week and Ingrid has a rotten respiratory infection.

I suspect that there is so much sickness now because children have returned to school and are swapping bugs back and forth. All of the Unit's personnel have kids and many of our patients are children. None of these illnesses are serious, but the possibility that one might become so is scary. I asked the AGBU to send flu vaccine; the Unit's personnel should all take it. Dr. Vigen Darian arrives Friday and I hope that he will bring it with him. He will also, I hope, bring my return ticket.

A joke from army days (fifty years ago this year!) surfaced from cerebral depths as I typed the line above. A soldier began to act strangely. He wandered around in a daze, apparently searching for something. He refused to follow orders, and kept repeating, "Where is it? Where is it?" Army psychiatrists exmined the man but were unable to explain his bizarre psychosis. His condition worsened. He became increasingly disoriented and his only words were, "Where is it? Where is it?." He was finally given a "Section 8" mental discharge. When an officer handed him the papers he looked them over carefully and then said, "*there* it is," and walked off into civilian life. When Vigen Darian hands me my ticket I'll know what to say.

Monday, 4 October 1993

On Saturday night, I developed diarrhea and the worst shaking chill I have ever had. The whole bed shook. Finally, I called Armine, my hands shaking so hard that I could barely dial her number. She came down, rummaged around and found an "Armenian blanket" to put over me. It's the equivalent of a European eiderdown duvet, but instead of being filled with feathers, it is filled with hanks of raw wool. I had seen great mats of tangled wool hung over the balcony-rails of apartments, and now I know what they are for. It was heavy, but warm. I crawled under while Armine fixed me some "Armenian penicillin," tea made with a berry syrup and cognac. A miracle cure! The chill went away and I slept.

A fax from Cathy was waiting in the office this morning. Her trip was smooth, but they had long waits, first to board in Yerevan, and then on the ground while refueling in Russia. The plane landed at Sochi, a resort city on the Black Sea, and finally there was a long wait for their luggage in Paris. She managed to get a flight to Rome and thence to Athens on the same day. She enjoyed her visit, but was glad to be home, too.

Today we learned that the Director has assigned yet another doctor to the Unit, an older general surgeon. One of the two general surgical services closed and he now has nothing to do. I interviewed him and found that he has no interest whatsoever in plastic surgery. I called the Director's office. Of the four persons that he has assigned, only Artur Khocharian is acceptable. Word came back that Tamasian did not wish to discuss the matter with me—so much for settling our problems here—and referred my call to the Vice Director. That's OK, he's a reasonable man. In the end, however, he didn't know what to do either and finally he called Tamasian.

The outcome is that the woman and the surgeon who appeared this morning will not stay. The third person, Samvel, will remain to rotate through our service as part of his general surgical training. I'll settle for that. Meanwhile, the best trainee on the service is the intern, Karen Danielian, who very much wants to go into plastic surgery. He works hard, he's intelligent and eager to learn. We should encourage him. He could, in time, be a great asset to the Unit, particularly if he could get some training out of the country, either in the States or in Europe.

Moscow—and therefore Yerevan—has been in a ferment all week. Yeltsin and Parliament have been fighting and the hard-liners are holed up in the Parliament building. That most sensitive of all indicators, the exchange rate, has been bouncing around and reflects accurately events in Moscow. Because of the general unrest, the Director met with the department chiefs and told them that the operating rooms will close. The Armenians fear that fighting will spread to other CIS states. The hospital must conserve supplies, the Director says. What will we do if we can't operate? Should I plan to leave? Should we try to call off Dr. Darian's visit?

Shortwave reception was good when I got home this afternoon— not always so, as there is so much local interference. I learned that the Russian army has remained loyal to Yeltsin, and has stormed the Parliament Building. The intransigent parliament members have surrendered and soldiers have carried them away. There was street fighting, and there were casualties, but the fighting ended and Mr. Yeltsin came out on top. He says that he will hold free elections, first for parliament and then for the presidency. On this basis, the countries of Europe and the US have pledged their support. I hope that he can pull it off. Anarchy in Russia would be hell. The Armenians seem to favor Yeltsin, although I gather that nobody feels very forceful about it. They do consider him to be a great improvement over Gorbachev, whom they hate. They believe that Gorbachev could have solved the Karabakh problem easily, and, because he did not, an interminable war with Azerbaijan resulted. Armenians don't understand why we in the West have a high regard for Gorby. The Cold War evidently was not as pervasive an entity here as it was in the West.

Karabakh is quiet now and we have not had any fresh casualties for a while. The doctors don't believe that the lull will last for long. Today we revised a below-the-knee stump on a young soldier whose leg was blown off by what Gagik calls a "bomb." From the nature of these traumatic amputations—we have seen quite a few—Gagik's "bombs" are anti-personnel mines. We had another war-related case today. The patient is a pleasant and stoic lady from Karabakh. She is in her mid-thirties and has a massive defect over her left scalp and temple, exposing an expanse of underlying bone. She was, she told us, one of thirty people in a gathering when a "bomb" (probably a mortar shell) landed in their midst. Ten were killed outright, she was one of the wounded. We covered the defect very nicely with a rotation scalp flap and skin grafted the donor area. Later on, if she wants, a tissue expander can be used to stretch the remaining hair-bearing scalp and replace the skin grafted area. As seems typical of the war injured that we care for, she is an excellent patient and appreciative of our care.

Another nagogram arrived this morning. It was only four pages long, but included no less than fifteen demands. A typical request was for dates, topics, subjects presented and the attendees for all the lectures and in-service presentations given by US and Armenian PRSC staff. That's an easy one. I have a lecture scheduled on microsurgery next week, other-wise there have been none. No problem, anyhow, we filed the fax.

Tuesday, 5 October 1993

Today we did a reduction cheiloplasty (correction of a fat lip) on one patient, reconstructed a thumb joint on another, and put a skin graft on the back of a hand and thumb on a third. Meanwhile, more strange things are happening. The Director called Artur Khocharian at his home late last night. He told Artur that as soon as I leave, he would be transferred back to Microsurgery. Further, he told Artur that he was going to ruin the PRSC. Was he drunk? Or just crazy?

Gagik met yesterday with the AGBU's lady President and the Direc-tor of the Erebuni Hospital, Yerevan's municipal hospital. It's obvious that the Unit can't remain at the Mikaelian Institute. The Erebuni director wants us to move there. If we move, he promises to remodel and dedi-cate two hospital floors to plastic surgery. Gagik says that he absolutely will not remain at the Surgical Institute unless Tamasian leaves. And that isn't going to happen.

Wednesday, 6 October 1993

I'm getting antsy, now that departure time approaches. I called Barbara to ask her to meet me in Paris. I want to be on my way.

Yesterday, as I was struggling to shape bone ends during a thumb joint reconstruction, I said that I wished we had power equipment. Artur Khocharian, who has very little English, said "Stryker drill" (a standard power instrument used for drilling and shaping bone.)

"Yes, a Stryker drill," I said, "that's what I want. We don't have one."

"Stryker drill! Yes, Stryker drill." Artur replied.

"Where?" I asked, "in the microsurgery department?"

"No microsurgery. Here!"

First I'd heard of it. I asked Jayne. She knew nothing about it, either. Then, after looking around, she found a foot pedal and cable for the drill. After I finished the operation, I checked with Mishak the Unit's engineer. He has what is left of the instrument. A nurse had broken it six months earlier and it had never been repaired or replaced. Mishak identified the broken part, and sent several faxes to New Jersey, copies of which he pulled out of his files to show me, asking for replacement parts. A message came back, saying in essence: "Have the drill repaired in Yerevan." Ice cubes in hell again. Mishak eventually gave up and there the matter ended and the Unit was left without a valuable piece of equipment. Each time Jayne and I find out about another broken or non-functional item—and there are so many now that Mishak's office looks like a surgical junkyard—Mishak produces copies of the pertinent correspondence asking for help. Vigen Darian arrives in two days. He expects to do maxillofacial reconstructive cases. He will want a power drill. We'll see what we can cobble up or borrow from another department.

The situation in Moscow has cooled down. Nevertheless, our driver, Gagik's cousin Artur, told us today that the value of the ruble continues to plummet. Whenever there is a hint of trouble, hard currency—the American dollar and the German deutschmark—increases in value.

Yesterday, Ingrid and Jayne visited Erebuni Hospital. The hospital's director is thirty-seven years old and a medical school classmate of Gagik's. He has attracted several hospital specialty units that are subsidized by foreign service organizations, including a Center for Women's Reproductive Health sponsored by Harvard University and the Beth Israel Hospital in Boston. He has inaugurated educational programs, arranged for doctors to visit from abroad, and otherwise acted like a progressive and responsible hospital administrator. It makes sense for the AGBU to move there. There are other things to recommend it, beyond getting out from under Tamasian's thumb. First, Erebuni Hospital has a modern French dental unit and that would enhance the Unit's ability to treat cleft palate patients. Next, they have no microsurgical facility. Given our Unit's strength in that discipline, it would add to Erebuni's surgical capabilities and do away with the rivalry that exists here between the PRSC and the Microsurgical Department. Finally, the Erebuni Hospital's director has proven organizational ability and he might help to solve some of the Unit's management problems.

Thursday, 7 October 1993

Yesterday we revised the stump of the young man who stepped on a mine in Karabakh. We had four more cases scheduled, but the hospital's water supply went off and didn't come back on until afternoon. We were late getting started and we finished late in the evening. The other services are not operating at all because of the troubles in Moscow.

Tamasian called Gagik this morning and told him that he has transferred Artur Khocharian back to the Microsurgical service. By now it is
obvious that Artur, an excellent surgeon, is a valuable asset. Gagik pro-
tested. Tamasian denies that he ever ordered Artur to come to Plastic
Surgery in the first place. Gagik says that he saw the order. The Director's
office claims that they have no record of such an order. Tamasian is
either lying or playing mind games. After a bit of searching, Gagik found
the original copy. Now he has decided that if matters can't be resolved
satisfactorily, there will be no more surgery,. I'm bemused by all of this,
but mostly I'm plain fed up with Armenian hospital politics. Patients
admitted for surgery have been waiting for days, although that doesn't
seem to bother anyone. We now have waiting in the hospital, a free flap,
facial reconstruction for Romberg's hemifacial atrophy (the last of three),
a hypoglossal-to-facial nerve crossover for facial nerve paralysis that I
want to do, the result of a gunshot wound to the mastoid region, and a
half dozen burn reconstructions. There are also many facial reconstructive cases waiting for Dr. Darian who arrives tomorrow.

Friday, 8 October 1993
Vigen Darian arrived this morning and will stay for a month. He is engaging, knowledgeable, and, I presume, competent. His father came from
Yerevan—so Vigen has many relatives here—then moved to Persia (Iran)
and finally to America when Vigen was a child. Vigen looks Armenian,
he could be Karen Manvelyan's brother. Although he speaks Armenian
slowly, nobody seems to have trouble understanding him. Gagik says that
he has a pronounced Persian accent. With such a background, his time in
Armenia should be a splendid experience.

The Vice-Minister of Health showed up this morning and met with
the surgeons in the outer office. There was a lot of noisy discussion.
Later, I met with him briefly and voiced the usual platitudes: how well the
Unit was doing, how the quality of surgery was excellent, how badly
needed the Unit is. There were problems, I said, but these could all be
solved with little difficulty, except for the hospital director. He seems to
be the victim of a personality disorder. Gagik hesitated before translating. Armenians really do have trouble with the power structure, unlike
brash Americans. Later, I talked about our meeting with Karen Manvelyan.
Karen is smart and has common sense. He laughed and said, "Nothing
will happen. These people are politicians and they will do nothing. You'll
find that this man is the same as all the others." He's probably right.

Next week will be my last whole week of surgery, and then, after the
weekend, there will be only three days more. Jayne Prentice says I have

the short-timer's syndrome, a condition she calls "the shorts," a 'Nam service term for the euphoria that sets in when the end is in sight.

Saturday, 9 October 1993

I am irked that we were operating today. Gagik wants to make up for the time that we lost. There are so many things that I would like to do: get my ticket at the travel agency, go to Vernissage one last time to look for souvenirs, buy tins of caviar to take home, and look for last photo opportunities. No chance to do any of these things today. Further, Gagik scheduled the cases badly. He wanted both to do an operation for syndactyly in a child and to help Vigen do a rhinoplasty. I worked in the smaller OR and did a composite graft for a nasal defect. (A composite graft includes not only skin but underlying soft tissue and cartilage. When used for nasal reconstruction the graft is usually taken from the rim of the ear.) I finished hours before the others, so rode home with Gagik's cousin Artur. Jayne called me later to find out what was happening. She hadn't gone to the hospital.

"If they can cancel cases during the week for no reason," she said, "I don't see why I should have to work on Saturday."

She's right, for there was no good reason to cancel surgery. Gagik's excuse was that he was "not psychologically ready." I had hoped to get out with my camera, but it was too late when I got home. Yerevan is not a place that calls for color film. The city and its people are drab. Once one takes the standard, postcard-type snaps of Republic square and the important buildings and monuments, one has to hunt for color. There are no worn doorways with fading bright paint, no sunny flower-filled windows, no colorful clothes hung out to dry that one sees in the Mediterranean countries—Italy, Greece, France—and in Central and South America. Here, people wear dull clothing and the only splashes of color dotting the city-scape are rugs airing, draped over the apartment balcony railings and in Vernissage. Children's clothes also put a bit of color on the streets, but there are few children in downtown Yerevan. The middle aged and the old predominate. When I see children, they are walking hand-in-hand with parents or grandparents. Many of the parents seem much older than one would expect them to be.

Rebecca West, writing about Macedonia, took note of how the Turks aged prematurely. Not, she believed, a somatic aging, for middle-easterners tend to be long lived. Rather, it is a psychologic aging, although she suspected that there was a genetic component, one that strikes men at about thirty-five, an age that coincides with the assumption of responsible administrative duties. She believed that the Turkish inability to govern the

Balkans effectively was the result of middle age slowing of thought. Right or not, I imagine that I see this here. There is little spontaneity, little gaiety (admittedly there is little reason for either, but still...). Here, the middle aged seem stolid, inexpressive, and turned off. How much of this is due to the effects of Dame West's theory, how much to present circumstances, and how much to the stultifying effects of seventy years of communism, I can't say. Maybe all of the above. I wonder, too, whether there is an element of natural selection. Have those blessed with pioneer spirit left Armenia, leaving behind others less driven and creative?

Byzantine peoples, and those of the middle east, revel in the detailed and the convoluted in their art and architecture, but I see little expression of this on Yerevan's streets. One must visit museums, the better shops, or Vernissage, to find it. There one can find examples of technical virtuosity that reveal infinite patience and love of detail: intricate carving, exquisitely wrought reproductions of the illuminations of the manuscripts of the Matenadaran, landscapes made from the petals of flowers, shavings of wood, and even leaves of straw. Much is kitsch, but there are also examples which show painstaking attention to minutia, typical of the best of Armenian crafts. Meticulosity in art is not a latter day phenomenon. The *khachkars*, "cross-stones," of which there must be hundreds in Armenia, and the exquisite sculptures and bas-reliefs associated with church architecture, show that Armenian's love for the intricate goes back a thousand years.

The khachkars are fascinating examples of Armenian skill and devotion in the execution of incredible detail. These holy stone tablets—most are about five feet high—are found in and around many of the early churches and graveyards. They have central palmate crosses which often stand on a circular emblem reminiscent of the Chinese yin and yang. Some also depict saints or religious scenes. Their backgrounds are usually laceworks of repeating cords and convoluted knots with no beginning and no end, representing the infinity of redemption. They seem to be unique to Armenia.

The cross was used as a symbol during the earliest days of the Armenian Church. Religious sites that were originally pagan were marked with stone crosses when they became Christian, but the khachkars did not appear until the ninth century and then evolved over the next millenium. Found primarily in religious settings, they were also used "to commemorate military victories, immortalize historically important events, and to commemorate the completion of churches, fountains, bridges and other constructions ... to repress or moderate the drought, the hail, the eartquake, etc. ... khachkars [were] erected in memory of sacrificed heroes, [and] unfortunate lovers." (from *Armenian Khachkars*, Yerevan, Editions Erebouni, 1978).

Sunday, 10 October 1993

Today we returned to Echmiadzin with Vigen Darian. Jayne and Ingrid's friend, Tigran, drove us in his falling-apart Volga. We stopped first to attend the service at St. Hripsemeh's church, and then went on to the cathedral in Echmiadzin. The young seminarian who had showed us around before was waiting in the museum. He had said that he would show us the church's treasury, located in another building, but he could not (somebody isn't there on Sunday, etc.) While waiting, I bought a book on the sacred architecture of Armenia, published under the auspices of the Church. The photography is excellent and inclusive. I'm not a religious person and I can't explain why the history of the Armenian church—its services, architecture, and sculpture—fascinates me. My visits to ancient religious sites have been the most agreeable aspect of my stay.

After the service, we dallied in the sun. I walked around the grounds, photographing khachkars set in the walls, and a bas relief genocide monument. The grounds surrounding the Echmiadzin cathedral are beautifully kept. It is as attractive a place as one will find here.

Armenians are among the world's most hospitable people. Several elderly women grounds-workers sat in the sun eating bread, cheese, and fruit. They insisted—it would have been insensitive to refuse—that we share their food. So they divided their bunches of grapes and that was our lunch.

Yet another ancient church, St. Gayane's, is nearby. It was built in 630 A.D., twelve years after St. Hripsemeh's. It has a wide porch, wider than the church itself, with three large arched entrances. It, like the porch of St. Hripsemeh's, was built much later. The porch ceiling is made of thin red bricks, and decorated with a well executed religous painting. The churchyard was filled with children playing, dressed in their Sunday best. The girls wore the brightest, reddest, shiniest shoes I've ever seen. They are imported from China. Later, Armine told me that she bought several pairs for Ala. She added that, while the shoes are attractive, they also wear out in two weeks.

We headed back toward Yerevan, stopping on our way at Zvartnots, a small community three kilometers from Echmiadzin, to visit the site of the Church of St. Gregory the Illuminator. It was built between 641 and 661 A.D. on the spot where St. Gregory met King Tiridates. It was the most ambitious of all of Armenia's many early churches. The building was round, with three concentric domes rising one above the other, supported by interior columns. (A large model of the completed church is in the National Museum. It shows its appearance and details of construction.) The church collapsed three centuries later in one of Armenia's frequent earthquakes.

Enormous chunks of rubble litter the site. Restoration has been going on, desultorily, for nearly a century, but the church is still in ruins. The base, a portion of the outer walls and a few central columns have been restored, but at the present rate, it will take at least another millenium before it will resemble the original structure. It now functions as a stronghold for boys who play among the ruins.

Tigran, on our way back to Yerevan, tried to save gas by running the car up to speed and then turning off the engine and coasting. For some reason he removed the key from the ignition lock. This not only locked the steering wheel, but the amount of gas saved by this asinine maneuver is minuscule. Then, catastrophically, he broke the key off in the ignition as he prepared to re-start the engine. Now he could not turn the steering wheel and we were committed to a predetermined trajectory. Luckily, this deposited us on the right side of the road where, since we were close to the airport, there are many kiosks selling liquor, cigarettes, and candy. There we were; the motor was not running, the key was broken off in the ignition switch, and the steering wheel was locked. We bought beer at a kiosk. Since good luck had deposited us there, it seemed to be the right thing to do. Almost immediately a circle of on-lookers gathered around us, all giving advice. The tendency for Armenians to gather and to give advice is a recognized national trait. When I remarked on this later to Armine, she laughed and then asked me why nobody had ever been raped in Republic Square. Her answer was that it would be impossible; too many people would gather to give advice on how to do it.

We drank our beer and wondered how we might get out of our predicament. Finally, Vigen solved the problem by cutting the wires to the steering column. Then, watching the ammeter, he hot-wired the car. I was impressed. Vigen comes from Detroit.

Meanwhile, Tigran retrieved a wrench from a trunk filled with standard Armenian auto survival gear: tools, water, oil, a jerrican of gas, rags, wire, sparkplugs, assorted nuts and bolts, fan-belts, and other automotive miscellany. He removed the ignition switch from the steering column and this unlocked the steering wheel. So, after the usual push, we continued on our way back to Yerevan. Driving in Armenia is too exciting. I'll ride to work, and I'll ride to the airport, but I don't care if I don't go anywhere else.

Tuesday, 12 October 1993

Yesterday, while Vigen saw patients, I helped Leon release an elbow contracture on an older lady. Then, since we were through by mid-afternoon, we left early. The nurses and Vigen wanted to go to one of Yerevan's very few restaurants, the Cracow, for dinner. The meal was just OK: chicken, fried potatoes, lavash (of course), tomatoes, cucumbers and cheese. It only cost the equivalent of $7.50 for the four of us, so who's to complain?

Thursday, 14 October 1993

Yesterday was a screwed up day at the Surgical Institute. We did the last patient with Romberg's facial atrophy. I told the Armenians to do the case. They are card-carrying microsurgeons, and they have observed and helped with two similar patients.

Vigen assisted Gagik in doing the face-lift part of the procedure, while I helped Artur Khocharian dissect out a muscle from the back for transfer. I am again impressed with his surgical ability What an asset he would be for the PRSC if he remained with the Unit! When we finished taking the muscle, Gagik and Vigen were still working on the face, so I went into the other OR and removed a vascular tumor from a woman's face. When I returned, Gagik was carrying on about the size of the facial vessel which he said was too small. I scrubbed and found that he had divided the artery. Further, it was at least three millimeters in diameter, more than adequate size.

Now, the vessel had been cut too short and Gagik couldn't attach the blood vessels to the muscle flap. I closed the wound on the back and rescrubbed while Artur tried to anastomose (attach) the vessels of the muscle to the short facial artery stump. Because he had to work end-on with a very short end, he couldn't complete it either. Eventually, I T-ed the incision into the woman's neck and found the continuation of the facial artery. Artur then was able to do the anastomosis successfully. The muscle was without circulation for five hours. It will probably survive, but I wouldn't be surprised if we lose it.

I was angry. They should have known that the vessel was large enough and not divided it until they knew where the anastomosis would be. So, because of a late start, bad judgement, fooling around, watching the flap, etc., we got home after 10:00 pm., the latest yet. I hope that this was my last big case in Armenia. I have some ordinary, medium sized operations to do, and then I can get organized for leaving. What bothers me most about today's screw-up is that if I had dissected the vessel in the first place, the case would have been routine.

Friday, 15 October 1993

Now for the ongoing saga of the facial flap . . . .

Yesterday morning when we made rounds it looked OK, but Artur Khocharian came in late and when he saw it an hour later, it did not seem to be perfusing. So, we returned the lady to the OR where he and Leon explored the wound (after waiting for the water to come back on; it was off for two hours). The artery had clotted. He reestablished circulation —Artur is the true hero of this case—we gave her heparin (an anti-clotting agent). Then we drained 700 cc of blood out of her back where we had taken the muscle (the wound had been totally dry when we closed it!) While they were doing this I removed a large benign tumor from the root of the arm on an older lady.

Today, Friday, the flap lady really looked peaked. Much discussion about transfusion. Her hematocrit (a measure of the amount of circulating red blood cells) was low, but I do not trust anything that comes out of the hospital lab. Everyone except Gagik was against transfusion if her hematocrit held. Later, they told me, that it had fallen to 10, which, if true, is the lowest I have ever heard of in a surgical patient (a normal value for a woman would be about 38). They gave her washed red cells and albumen, to which she had a severe allergic reaction. Whew! She seems to be all right now, but we'll see. [*Happily, she did very well and the transferred tissue survived.*]

I re-operated on the little girl with the severely burned neck. The original thin split-thickness graft contracted, as I had feared. This time Karen M. gave her some ketamine (an injectable sedative) anesthesia. I infiltrated the high neck with dilute xylocaine and epinephrine, cut her throat and he put in the endotracheal tube. Again we opened her neck and chin area up very widely and corrected her drooping lower lip simultaneously, using thick skin grafts for the neck and a full thickness skin graft for her face, and carefully sutured it all down. It looked fine and, if the graft takes, it may be adequate. While we were doing this, Vigen closed a large cleft palate with Leon. By then the hospital had run out of oxygen so we had to cancel the rest of the cases.

Back in the apartment, I worked on packing. I think that I can get everything home, because Barbara had sent an enormous military duffle bag. It will weigh a ton. What will I do with the two liter bottle of Armenian cognac that the hernia man gave me? [*No problem; I hand-carried it safely to Idaho.*]

Saturday, 17 October 1993

I walked downtown to the travel agency, arranged for my ticket, and met Karen Danielian, our intern. He had asked me to come to lunch to meet his mother. First, though, we went to the Hotel Ani and changed twenty five dollars into rubles. The rate is now three thousand rubles to the dollar; three times what it was when I arrived three months ago.

The Danielians live close to the opera house. Theirs is like every apartment in Yerevan, a bleak entry, broken windows, chipped and crumbling concrete stairs and walls, and then a pleasant and well furnished apartment. We were greeted by a shaggy, well-behaved cocker spaniel named "Lord" whose favorite food is apples. I asked whether dog food is available. Karen said that EuroVision advertises dog food, but there is none in Armenia so they make their own. Television channels like EuroVision and CNN are windows through which Armenians look out into a different world. I saw no heater or radiator in the apartment and asked how they made out last winter. Karen said that it had been incredibly cold, so cold that his mother's fingers were frostbitten. He shook his head as he described it, and said that it had been just awful.

His mother speaks little English, so we chatted through Karen. She is an ophthalmologist and works in the Ophthalmologic Institute. Theirs is a medical family and Karen is a fifth generation doctor. Again, I realized how frustrating the inability to speak a language can be, for she is an interesting woman and I would have liked to have talked with her directly. Later, Karen gave me a souvenir, a reproduction of a Matenadaran manuscript with a thoughtful letter thanking me for the teaching that I had done while I was here.

Lunch was delicious: cake, baked apple with walnuts, cognac, coffee, and a fruit juice that they make at their country house, twenty-five kilometers from Yerevan. (The recipe calls for one kilogram of blackberries or raspberries, and three liters of boiling sugar water; it makes a refreshing fruit drink.)

As we were leaving, Karen asked if I was interested in "chorches" (churches). I am, so we visited nearby St. Zorbaran, a tiny church nestled in a wooded area surrounded by high apartment buildings. It was built in 1694, which, for Armenia, makes it almost modern. A wedding was in progress. I took pictures of the bride and groom as they stood in the entrance. Then, on my way home, I stopped off at the cheese store to get some tins of caviar for Barbara and for gifts.

At 3:00 p.m., I crossed to the market for a pre-arranged meeting with the father of one of our patients, Henry Sarkissian. The Director had introduced me to Henry shortly after I arrived. Later, at the Director's request, Cathy and I had operated on his daughter, Aruz, the sixteen year old girl with the contracted ear deformity. The ear, fortunately, turned out quite well. I cared for the girl personally after her surgery, doing her dressings, removing sutures, etc. Henry had invited us to visit his house at the time. We were so busy that I put him off. Several days ago, he showed up and insisted that we visit. So, rather reluctantly—I still haven't finished packing—I agreed to go today.

His son drove. He is in his mid-twenties, muscular, with a short beard, heavy features, and the incredibly blue eyes that some Armenians have. Henry told me that he is a "sportsman" and a boxer (one never knows what an English term like "sportsman" means here). I was unable to find out what else, if anything, he does beside drive Henry around. Gagik followed in his car with Henry's other guests: Gagik's wife, Gohar; Ingrid and Jayne; and Vigen Darian. We climbed high above the city and stopped before a house mostly hidden behind a high fence. A beautiful dog, a boxer, greeted us. We entered the house through a garage in which stood a carousel-shaped machine. It was about sixteen feet in diameter, with large spindles of fine thread mounted every foot or so around its upper circumference. It was a loom, a computerized device that makes cloth from beginning to end, rolling the completed fabric onto a large roller at its base. Henry waited at the open door to the house and we caught a glimpse of the interior. The house was opulent.

"I'm going to buy one of those looms when I get back to Idaho," I whispered to Vigen. "It will fit in my garage and then I can get a house like this."

"I have a feeling that the machine is not responsible for the house." Vigen whispered back.

Our remarks were relayed to Henry who laughed and allowed that his real occupation was not making cloth, the loom was a hobby. Henry is a "businessman" which, like "sportsman" is an ambiguous term. It could mean anything. For all I knew, we were walking into Mafia Central.

Henry, his house, his loom and his family were a side of Armenia, of which I had seen little. I met Henry's wife in the hospital when she cared for Aruz. She is a quiet, composed, attractive lady. She does not look Armenian, nor does Henry. Their house is completely different from any I have seen here. The floors are fine parquet. The entry and stairs are marble. The spacious living and dining areas are well furnished and many fine oil paintings hang on the walls. A large painting in the dining area was an eye-catcher. From the style and the crazing of the paint I guessed it dated from the 1870s. Henry said it was German. I liked it a lot, as much for the content as for the artistic capabilities of the artist, although these were more than adequate. The painting depicted a moonlight scene of a lush, reclining nude in a sylvan setting. The artist had carried it off well.

Armenian custom does not include wasting time with preliminaries, so we sat down at a long dining table almost as soon as we arrived and dinner started immediately. Henry served cognac from an unlabeled bottle. It was, he said, ninety three years old, distilled and barrelled in 1900. The others said that they could tell that it was smoothly different. I could not taste much difference between this and other fine cognacs, such as "Nairi," which is "only" thirty years old. Nairi (Nah-EERY) is my favorite of the Armenian cognacs and Henry poured that after we finished the first bottle.

Lavash was at every plate. There were several salads; one was similiar to Greek tsatziki (yogurt, garlic, cucumber) and herbs. Other dishes held spiced meats, bastromah and tzutzuki. Then, platters of boiled lamb appeared. Now the toasts began in earnest with Gagik translating. The first toast was to the missing person, Cathy Vlastou. The chair opposite Henry remained empty in her honor. Catherine had made an indelible impression on every Armenian who met her; our surgeons and Armine have not stopped talking about her. Karen Manvelyan, whenever he mentions her, always adds "the best surgeon I've ever seen." I respond, "Karen, the best *woman* surgeon you've ever seen." He comes back with, "No, the best *surgeon* I've ever seen." He may be right.

The toasts continued. To me. I did the best I could to respond. Next, Henry toasted Vigen with an earnest, moving, and heartfelt tribute to the Armenians who had left Armenia, but who had really never left. All eyes were moist. Kleenex time. Then more toasts. To Armenian-American friendship, to American nurses, to each guest, and there were many. To women, and then a toast to all children, including ourselves. When we got to the children, I knew that it was getting late. I hadn't moved from my seat and when I did, I realized that I was starting to get—for the first time in many years, sozzled. Fortunately at this point Henry decided to take us on a tour of his house: the billiard room, the swimming pool (no water), the sauna, the greenhouse (no plants), and a finished attic with a great view of Yerevan from the roof.

Then, back to the table, more goddam toasts. A big kiss from Henry and then time to go. As we went I felt Henry slip something into my shirt pocket. I tried to return whatever it was, but by now I was fairly helpless. And so we left.

Gagik and Henry helped me up the stairs to the apartment, which was a good thing. I took my clothes off and remembered to check the item in my shirt pocket. Jewelry. Unwrapped, in the store's cellophane envelope. Armenians don't wrap gifts, they just give them. There was a heavy gold man's ring with an obsidian stone and a small diamond for me. There were two gold earrings in a trefoil design with a diamond setting, for Catherine. It was too much. We had visited Henry's house.

Sunday, 18 October 1993

I got up late. Surprisingly, no hangover. I know that Armenian cognac is good, but built-in morning-after protection also also seems to be a favorable attribute. After breakfast I walked down to Vernissage, looking for the nurses and Vigen. They weren't there, or I missed them, so I walked home to get ready for a christening party for Karen Manvelian's daughter, Christina.

Before leaving Vernissage, I bought two more old cameras, a very worn Contax 1A, and a Fed, another Russian knock-off of an early Leica. Later, I found that the Contax was not in great shape. I think that I paid too much for it. [*So I thought at the time, but in the States I sold it for five times as much as I paid.*] The Fed is a very nice pre-war camera with an uncoated collapsible lens, lens cap, and a five digit serial number. The body is covered with fine glove leather. The workmanship is good, but not up to that of the Leica II from which it was copied.

At 3:00 Gagik came to take us to St. Sarkis's church for the christening. Karen's wife Irena, "Ira," (pronounced "Eera") is Belarusan, and a gynecologist. She is an attractive blonde lady with the petite nose and broad cheekbones of a Baltic Russian. Karen told Cathy during her visit, that Ira does not like Armenia and returned now only for the christening. Karen would very much like to go to Belarus to be with his family, especially as he was separated so long from them while he was in the States. Of the original cadre, Karen is the one most likely to leave Armenia if he can find the opportunity to do so. If he doesn't stay, he will be joining the twenty percent or so of the population who have left the country, driven away by hard times, another diaspora.

The separation that the AGBU imposed on the trainees bothers me even more, now that I have met their families. Vigen says that the organization did not send the families for fear of defection. Maybe so, or perhaps he is excusing the organization's meanness, for he is quick to defend the AGBU. In any event, it was an unpleasant year for the trainees. Now Karen is trying to figure out some solution to his dilemma. He asked Cathy to find out whether he could emigrate with his family to Greece. He is a good anesthesiologist, and would do well anywhere. [*In the fall of 1995, I received a call from Karen. He was working as a technician in a laboratory in San Francisco and asked if I could recommend him. I could, of course. His family remained in Belarus. He hoped to have them join him in the States. Whether he will ever be able to function as an anesthesiologist in the States is up in the air.*]

The christening was in a small chapel. The priest was young, bearded, and very competently sang the entire ceremony. I understood nothing, of course, beyond the "Alleluias" and "Amens" that are part of every Christian service. Gagik and Gohar were god-parents and they gave the child a large doll, and a gold cross and chain. The christening was not by immersion, but still wet enough that the priest wrapped the child in a towel beforehand. At the close, he anointed the child's body generously with oil which may not be washed off for three days. Then, in another ceremony, the child will be bathed.

We went now to the Manvelian's apartment where his family and friends were gathered. The meal consisted of many salads, each of which had a dominant vegetable: eggplant, cabbage, beet, potato, beans and so on. These were followed with fish baked in lavash. I tried to pass on this, having had several meals of Lake Sevan fish, filled with nasty little bones and not at all tasty. Gohar persuaded me to try one. It was completely different from those that I had eaten earlier. It was tasty, pink and nearly boneless; it was trout! I had read of Lake Sevan trout; now I know that there is such a thing. Next came randomly cut chunks of boiled lamb, served with ketchup. Armenians love ketchup and at the other end of the table I saw Mishak pouring it on his bread and enjoying it greatly.

Gagik was tamadah, and as always, we drank a prodigious amount. Even though we ate a lot of food, it is possible to drink too much, as I found out last evening. Tonight, common sense and restraint prevailed and aside from a pleasant glow, the vodka had little effect.

Monday, 18 November 1993
The hospital has no oxygen, so we can do only local procedures. I removed a large morpheaform basal cell cancer from just above the brow, on a middle-aged lady pediatrician. There was, of course, no frozen section control, nor had there been a preliminary biopsy. Vigen was upset. He felt that both were necessary in treating such a condition. He will learn, as I did, that if these localized cancers are adequately and aggres-

sively resected, preliminary biopsy and frozen section—while nice to have—are not necessary. Wide resection should be curative for this lesion. Basal cell carcinomas recur because surgeons are afraid that they will not be able to close the defect that remains after a wide resection. Therefore, they stay too close to the margins of the growth and recurrences are common. I suspected the diagnosis when I had seen her originally, but under the OR lights it was typical of a "wildfire" spreading growth, with a flat center and low edges. I removed it with generous margins. It is unlikely that it will recur. Now, I was left with a very large hole. After considering various alternatives, I used a rotation flap carried up to the hairline. With wide undermining of adjacent forehead, this worked very well. Samvel assisted me, and he asked over and over again, "Can I sew, Dr. Earle, can I sew?"

I was provoked. I was trying to close a large facial defect on a lady physician, carefully adjusting suture placement and tension, tailoring a dog-ear here, removing tissue from the end of a back cut there. I did not need a person who has had three months of surgery to nag me to let him sew. I was also irked that none of the other surgeons looked in as I did the case. The ability to reconstruct large defects sets plastic surgeons apart from other surgical specialists, and they would have learned from this case.

When I was done, Artur drove the two American nurses, Vigen, and me to the opposite side of the city to keep an appointment with the director of the Erebuni Hospital. We were late, because of my surgery, but still had almost an hour and a half to talk with him, and then to tour the facility. Vigen monopolized the Director throughout and that bothered Armine (who translated, *sotto voce*, as we walked along), for Vigen spoke with great authority, saying things that did not at all agree with what the AGBU's President had told us earlier. I said nothing for these are matters for the future. At the end, Gagik summed up for us in English what the Director had said. Namely, if the Unit moves to Erebunit the hospital will give it temporary bed space and an operating room to use for two months while they remodel a floor. The Unit's facilities, the director said, would be comparable to those which it presently has.

The nurses and Vigen were adamant that the new Unit must have oxygen and suction in every room, American furnishings, special nursing facilities, and on and on. I felt, and said, that they are not taking into account two things. First, this is Armenia. Second, and more importantly, they are not thinking about the nature of plastic surgery. In the States, most plastic surgical cases are not even admitted to the hospital and the majority of those who are admitted are not high risk patients. The AGBU should consider this, and should delineate the Unit's aims for the future. If patients require oxygen, suction, monitoring, special nursing care, etc., they can be admitted to the main hospital. Erebuni has skilled intensivists, nurses and a modern ICU, as we saw on our tour.

Going first class, American style, is an expensive luxury. The Plastic and Reconstructive Center's initial goal was to provide reconstructive plastic surgical care for the victims of the 1988 earthquake. Apparently as AID money became available, the objective expanded and permitted replication of an American university's plastic surgical facilities in Yerevan. As a consequence, the PRSC is weighed down with broken, inoperative, inappropriate, duplicated, unused, and expensive high tech equipment. If the Unit is relocated, why repeat prior mistakes? Practically, however, I suspect that unless the AGBU can float another AID grant, financial considerations will temper excess and favor common sense.

The AGBU's focus should be on training surgeons, rather than on a plant and its equipment. If there are good plastic surgeons, there will be good plastic surgery. Further, flying surgeons to Armenia for two or three week stints should be done for teaching purposes, rather than for service. Basic plastic and reconstructive services should be provided by PRSC staff surgeons, not by a sequence of visiting docs.

The Erebuni hospital and its director impressed me. First, the facility is not under the Armenian Ministry of Health. It is a municipal hospital, and answers to the Mayor and the City of Yerevan. Next, there are already other services supported from overseas, including the Harvard-Beth Israel Women's Reproductive Service, and the French Dental Service that I had heard about earlier. We visited the latter unit. It is a well planned, modern facility. The equipment is not the gleaming free-form ceramic and plastic equipment one sees in dentists' offices in the States. It is simple and practical field equipment. Mark up one for the French.

Finally, the hospital is seething with construction activity. The director showed us pictures of what it had been only two years ago: rubble filled halls and unfinished rooms. He gets things done.

"What do you think?" Gagik asked me later.

"I think that the AGBU should cut its losses, salvage whatever it can from the Surgical Institute, and move right now," I replied.

"It's not that simple" Gagik said, shaking his head. "Hamlet doesn't want the Unit to leave the Surgical Institute."

"Of course he doesn't," I replied, "he's having too much fun jerking you guys around."

Gagik nodded. If he didn't understand what I said, he knew what I meant.

A long day, but not over yet. Ingrid, in her capacity of nurse manager, had arranged a tour of the Yerevan Cognac Factory. It wasn't easy to arrange, but she is resourceful and told them that "world famous visiting surgeons (Vigen and I) wanted to see how cognac is made in Armenia." So Ingrid, Jayne, Vigen and I went on our tour.

The Cognac Factory is an enormous complex made up of innumerable low, solid, red brick buildings. We passed security personnel at the gate and emerged into a large courtyard. Several long tank trucks filled with raw brandy, distilled elsewhere, were being emptied. Now I realize why a country which has so many vines has so little wine; the juice goes into cognac. As we watched, some of the raw liquor sloshed out of the trucks and puddled onto the ground. I had to turn my head.

A junior administrator showed us around. We saw gleaming stills that emptied into holding vats and thence into great tuns for aging. There are, he said, 11,000 barrels in the factory, some are large enough to park an auto inside and all are filled with cognac. The liquor is moved from barrel to barrel through pipes and hoses for blending. The factory makes fourteen different blends. The cognac is then aged from a few, to twenty or thirty years, or even longer, as with Henry's ninety-three year old bottle. The blends, sold under different labels, vary in taste, age, and obviously, in price.

We visited a room where white clad workers stood around a long table, preparing presentation cut-glass bottles. It was a real cottage enterprise. At the far end a lady filled the special crystal bottles, pouring the brandy into each one by hand, through a funnel. Next, a man and a woman filed corks to fit in the bottle necks, then banged them in with mallets. The next man sawed the top of each cork off flush with the bottle top. Finally, at the near end of the table, a group of ladies put foil around the tops and pasted on labels. The workers were friendly and seemed to enjoy our visit. The tour ended in a tasting room lined with presentation bottles and gift packs. We sampled a few glasses and then we all bought bottles of different kinds of cognac. The cognac here is more expensive than on the street. The personnel told us that here we get the real thing, whereas some cognac sold on the street is re-labeled with labels from higher priced varieties.

Artur was to meet us outside the factory at 5:00 p.m. No Artur. So we set out on a long march, down the hill above the Razdan, past the sports stadium, across the river, past St. Sarkis church, and because the

Big Mafia Restaurant is nearby, and because we were hungry, we stopped for supper: starters, beer, and their baked soup and bread. Then we walked up Mashdots Street, and turned right to the Hotel Armenia where I left the nurses and walked back to my apartment, the end of a long, full day.

Tuesday, 19 October 1993

Still no oxygen, so again we could do only local cases. I did a minor touchup on a secondary cleft lip that I had done earlier, revised an ear, and then a second stage flexor tendon reconstruction. It turned out that the tendon that we planned to use as a graft had been injured many years before and was not large enough. The opposite side was normal, but there was no tendon stripper (an instrument used to retrieve a tendon graft via a tiny incision) so retrieval was harder than it should have been. Then we didn't have the wires which are used for tendon repairs, so we had to improvise, all under local block anesthesia. It turned out all right, but I don't think that I would do another one under the same conditions. By then it was late. The Armenian staff had made plans for a last evening together. We went to a restaurant outside Yerevan. It wasn't good. By now we've seen so much of each other that the evening was anticlimactic and subdued.

Wednesday, 20 October 1993

I woke this morning feeling lousy, with diarrhea which steadily grew worse during the day. It is the fourth time that this has happened in Yerevan. Each time the diarrhea has responded to an antibiotic or Flagyl. I suspect last night's food. Between trips to the toilet I cleaned the apartment and finished packing my bags. Overall, they must weigh a hundred pounds or more, the most I've ever traveled with. We go to the airport at 1:30 a.m., and then I'm on my way to Paris.

Thursday, 22 October 1993

It has been three months to the day since I left Paris for Armenia. As expected, there was a long wait at the airport. All the doctors and the American nurses turned out to say goodby. Kisses and hugs and long goodbyes. The plane, a newer and much cleaner Tupolev 154 was loaded and, improbably, took off on time. The flight to Paris was smooth and uneventful. I thought about Armenia during the flight. I might have been on another planet. Among its many paradoxes are the differences in be-havior and achievement of Armenians in their landlocked little country and those in the outside world. In Armenia they necessarily devote their energy to low-level getting by. Graft, corruption, cronyism, nepotism, favors and payback are part of life; the goal is survival. The country is poor. It lacks power, electricity, and water, yet Armenians, at least those who live in Yerevan, are not poor. There is a 50% unemployment rate, but there seems to be plenty of money. Luxuries are available and lines wait to purchase them.

Remove Armenians to the west. They bloom. They soak up knowledge, work hard, and become valued members of their communities. Why do immigrants—not just Armenians—blossom in their new land? Our land. Because the aggressive and ambitious migrate? Or because the second generation, especially, was never exposed to the pervasive Soviet ethos? In Armenia there is little reward for achievement or for quality workmanship. Work is shoddy and buildings crumble. Employment does not depend on quality, and there is little material incentive. In the west, opportunity, education, chance of advancement, reward for achievement are built into the system. It was revealing for me to meet the doctors and nurses of Armenia. I suspect that under our system they would be aggressive performers in the mold of Armenian-Americans.

I'm not sorry to leave Armenia. To be there was, whatever else, an experience, one that I do not regret. Nevertheless, I'm ready for American home cooking! *

---

*While the preceding account relates primarily to the AGBU's role in founding and supporting the Yerevan Plastic and Reconstruction Center., readers should be aware that the AGBU provides services to Armenians throughout the world, as well as to those who reside in the Republic of Armenia. There, the AGBU supports educational programs, cultural organizations and events, and medical facilities; it also provides humanitarian aid to the needy, and has been active in an ambitious program to construct and restore Armenian holy sites.

Return to Armenia

27 April - 9 May 1995

The Plastic and Reconstructive Surgical Center moved to the Erebuni Hospital during the late fall and winter of 1993-4. It did not reopen until October, 1994, almost a year later. In the spring of 1995, the AGBU asked me to return to Yerevan. I had done no surgery during the year. The AGBU representative asked whether it would be possible for Dr. Catherine Vlastou to visit at the same time to back me up and act as primary surgeon during a twelve day visit. Cathy agreed and I met her in Athens.The flight, on an Armenian Airline Tu-154 (inherited from Aeroflot) from Athens to Yerevan was four hours late. It took more than three hours to retrieve our luggage and pass through Armenia's passport and customs control—longer than our flight. Old habits die hard and paranoid officialdom was much in evidence. Custom officials searched every bag, and recorded every bit of currency and every piece of jewelry for all passengers.

We finally emerged from the airport's dark concrete corridors in the early morning hours. Gagik, Armine, Leon, the two Karens (Manvelian and Danielian), and Marianne Hess who had returned to Armenia only a few days earlier, waited to greet us. Bottles of champagne popped as we celebrated our reunion. With few exceptions, the staff is as it was when I left in October of 1993. Artur Khocharian, regretfully, remained at the Mikaelyan Institute. Karen Danelian has now completed two years of surgical training, and is part of the permanent staff. Later, we found that the OR nurses, the ICU nurses, the floor nurses and the sanitars, were, almost without exception,ones with whom we had worked before. [*I mentioned this later to the pleasant and efficient lady who was working in the AGBU's New Jersey office. She remarked dryly that the American dollars that the AGBU pays the staff likely play a part in perpetuating this level of devotion.*]

Erebuni is the largest hospital in Armenia both physically and in number of beds. The hospital is a great pile, sheathed with pinkish-gray tufa. It is in poor repair, and large cracks, where the sheathing has fallen away, expose the building's underlying concrete skeleton. Inside, so much concrete has chipped away from the floors and stair risers that the unwary are in constant danger of falling. Otherwise, the facilities are similar to those that the Unit relinquished at the Surgical Institute: twenty beds in double rooms; two operating rooms (both sterilizers now work); with a recovery facility and ICU in the same corridor adjacent to the ORs, a far better arrangement than before. The biggest inconvenience, not a major one, is that the hospital is further from central Yerevan, making for a longer commute.

All of the doctors, at one time or another, asked me whether I thought that Yerevan had changed during the year and a half that we were away— they themselves did not think so. I told them that I saw many subtle changes that suggested that life in Armenia was improving. The fountains in Republic Square were now spurting water high in the air. They are brightly illuminated at night, and fill the square with subdued light. Most of Yerevan's roads are still deteriorating, but gaping potholes have been filled on a few of the city's streets, a tentative sign of recovery. Before, a few blocks from my apartment, the skeleton of a tall building under construction for the University of Yerevan was unfinished and abandoned, surrounded by rusting construction cranes. Work is now underway on the building and it is several floors higher. I mentioned this to little Ala on one of our evening walks. She opined that it was about time, after five years. And electricity and water availability are improved, but still iffy.

Tank trucks still park along Yerevan's streets, but there are now also mini-stations that dispense both regular and super gasoline. Fuel in Yerevan is considerably less expensive than in the States. Gagik says that this is a political thing. Russia sells the petrol at a low price to maintain good will within the CIS. More cars are on the streets, many are new four-wheel drive Nivas, similar to Fiat Pandas, that now come equipped with larger (1.7 liter) engines and gussied up interiors. The jeep-like Nivas, made in Russia, are well suited to Armenia's poor roads.

There are more stores and more items on sale. Vendors sell bakery products made from fine white flour on the downtown streets, whereas before only the traditional flat loaves, made from coarse, unrefined flour were available, and these were dispensed from government stores. The funicular that runs from below our apartment to the city's heights has been refurbished and is working. We saw a wide variety of imported fruits and produce for sale: kiwi fruit and oranges from Iran, candy and soft drinks from Turkey, toys from Russia, and clothes and other items from European countries. Our post-surgery snacks in the doctor's lounge (provided by grateful patient's families) now include Coca Cola bottled in the United Arab Emirates, imitation Coke from Iraq, Fanta orange drink from Turkey. And vodka—always vodka— from France, Germany, Holland, Sweden, and even from the United States (but not, for some inexplicable reason, from Russia where it may have been invented).

Before, quality soap and other kitchen and toilet items were not to be found, but now are easily available. We were amused to find that the Iranian dish soap that Armine gave us was brand-named "Barf," made in Iran. ("Barf," I learned, is "white" in Farsi, the modern Persian language.)

Construction of many new homes was the most striking evidence of change in the new Armenia, including architected luxury houses on large lots. We estimated that the cost of each house, if built in the United States or in Greece, would approach a million dollars. The doctors said that is just what they cost in Armenia, too, but that there is a difference. Here, a million American dollars represents a truly astronomical amount of money. The homes are being built by Armenia's nouveau riche, and paid for, presumably, with Armenian money. I pointed out that some good must come from the building spree. The money spent so ostentatiously and the related construction jobs had to benefit the general economy, an observation that did not impress the doctors.

The Unit seems to be functioning well. We saw a few cases, several with facial palsy, that we might have treated differently. Others, especially burn reconstructions, turned out well. I hoped that I would not have to operate, but there was so much to be done that I couldn't refuse, and we did thirty cases during our stay. It was more than the Armenians had done on their own during the previous three months. I was pleased to find that I still operated effectively. I was also glad that Catherine was there for backup. Many of the procedures were complicated and arduous: cancer resections, microsurgical reconstructive procedures, and other big cases.

We saw some of our former patients. We were pleased, for example, to see that the twenty-fingered child that we had operated on a year and a half ago, had done well and had an excellent result. After we examined her, her parents showed us her sister, born since our previous visit. Deja vu; she had almost identical deformities, so again we corrected both hands simultaneously.

We came under pressure to do cosmetic procedures. Cathy did a face-lift, a tummy tuck and thigh-plasty and I did several rhinoplasties. All were on doctors, nurses, or doctor's relatives. We were disturbed by this, for there were other patients whom we should have operated on, but could not because of time constraints. The Unit is supported and paid for by the AGBU, a charitable service organization. It was established to provide reconstructive surgery for those unable to obtain such care in Armenia. Should its resources be used to provide non-essential surgery to a favored few? The question keeps coming up and it needs to be addressed seriously by the AGBU, and by the Unit's doctors. The other side of the coin is that the Armenian docs are supposed to be plastic surgeons and they should be taught how to do cosmetic procedures.

Staff morale seems to be good. The Unit's worst problems were resolved by the move to Erebuni. The baleful influence of the Surgical Institute's Director is no longer an obstacle to the Unit's well being. I asked about the Director. He has, Armine told me, been made a professor of surgery in Yerevan's Medical School. What can one say, except to note that Armenia is Armenia. Most of the Unit's equipment problems were sorted out during the move. Those that remain, however, are troublesome. We often had to cancel or abort cases, because of electrical outages and loss of running water. I found out something that I really didn't want to know: it is possible to do a cleft lip repair using only the light provided by a pocket flashlight. Although the Unit has a small backup Briggs and Stratton generator supposedly capable of powering the OR's monitoring equipment, electrocautery, and emergency lighting, it seldom worked.

The highlight of our short visit was a final Sunday trip to the Khor Virap (the name means "dungeon") Monastery. It stands on a monadnock close to the Arax river, only a few yards from the Armenian-Turkish border. Legend says that St. Gregory the Illuminator was imprisoned in an underground hole here for thirteen years. The walled monastery is as close to Ararat as it is possible to get and still remain within Armenia's borders. It is a favorite subject of artists and photographers, pictured with the mountain looming in the background. The Armenian church, under the auspices of Catholicos Vazgen I, recently renovated the entire monastic complex. In addition to a large church and monastery buildings within the walls, there is a small, well worn, and ancient chapel. Its interior leather wall covering is so old that it seems to have become a petrified part of the underlying building blocks. Access to Gregory's underground keep is via a ladder located in a small vertical tunnel that descends deep into the underlying rock formation. I can believe that Gregory was imprisoned here, but that he survived in this hole for years, would be miraculous. Khor Virap is a popular spot, used for various rites of passage. Half a dozen weddings and several baptisms—some quite ostentatious—took place in rapid succession during our visit. It was strange for us to see a large party whose principle participant was a gaily groomed sacrificial goat, bedizened with colorful ribbons. Here, the place of animal sacrifice in the Armenian church is quite obvious. The priests sacrifice the animal, usually a chicken, and hold it up during its death flurries. The porch of the church is liberally spattered with animal blood.

Overall, our visit was both productive and enjoyable. Armenia remains, for me, a fascinating land.

Final Visit: Nagorno Karabakh

6-18 June, 1996

I returned again to Armenia in the late spring of 1996, arriving on a Friday afternoon. I had been asked, just before leaving the States, whether I wanted to go with the Unit's staff on a long-planned trip to Nagorno Karabakh. My answer was that I wanted to go so badly that I'd walk if that was the only way to get there.

We left early the following morning. There were, not counting our driver, eight of us in a large van: Gagik and his wife Gohar; Gohar's brother, Gagik Melikian, an official in the Armenian Security Service (known still as the KGB) and his fourteen year old son, Artur; Armine, and Emil, a junior anesthesiologist, new to the Unit since my last visit; Karen Danielian, and myself.

Once out of Yerevan, we headed south. On our right, high guard towers indicated the course of the Arax River and the Armenian-Turkish border. As long as we stayed on the peneplain the land was rich and under cultivation. Beyond, to the west, we saw the Armenian's "Macis" (Mt. Ararat). We passed through the towns of Artishat and Ararat, bleak communities whose blocky concrete buildings are their dominant feature. Miles later, the highway forked. The branch to the south, to the Azerbaijani enclave of Nakhichevan, was blockaded. Here, we turned east and climbed through treeless mountains to an 8000 foot summit before starting our descent. We were now in Zangezour, one of three disputed provinces. Nakhichevan, Zangezour, and Karabakh were all formerly populated by Armenians. Zangezour was the only one of the three incorporated into Armenia proper when the Bolsheviks annexed the Republic in 1922. Zangezour looks like the American West, Colorado, perhaps.

Our road followed a clear, rushing, tree-lined mountain stream. We came to a roadside market where we bought cheese and several yards of lavash. The browned sheets were as thin and soft as flannel. It was food, if needed, for the rest of the trip. A vendor was also selling red wine and insisted that we try some. It was surprisingly good, so we filled up an empty gallon-sized water bottle.

While we were visiting the different stalls, a white Lada sedan arrived and two plain clothes police officials emerged. The older man was the chief security officer for Siunik (I find it interesting that the name of the ancient kingdom persists), this region of Zangezour. He had been waiting for us, or, more accurately, waiting for Gagik Melikian, our Security man. When they met, they displayed a ritual of male bonding which I saw repeated over and over during the next three days, bear-hugs, kisses, prolonged hand holding: unlikely behavior in the West, but usual here. All of the Security personnel that we met, and we encountered many before our trip was over, knew one another. The KGB evidently is an elite fraternity.

I asked Karen why Armenians still refer to their country's Security Service as "KGB." Same organization, same personnel, same function, he told me, so why call it anything else? Curious, I asked whether the organization is as intrusive as it was under the Soviets. I didn't get a meaningful answer. In Armenia, I often feel like a person who admires water lilies without knowing what goes on in the turbid water below. [*An Armenian-American whom I met later understood my frustration. "Since you don't speak Armenian, you must have felt like a deaf man at a wedding," he said. It was a good analogy.*]

We followed the Lada for several miles to a riverside restaurant where a meal was waiting, the first of many that the KGB provided during the next few days: cold cuts, cucumbers, tomatoes, and plates of greens that included dill, parsley, basil, and a pungent herb that I did not recognize. "Tarkhoon," Armine told me. I sketched the leaves in my notebook. [*After I returned to the states I showed the sketch to my wife. "Why, it's tarragon, of course," she informed me. I should have guessed.*]

The main course was a carp-like, and very bony, fish from the nearby river. Clusters of bottles—soft drinks, cognac, wine, and vodka—stood on the table. There were the usual toasts, to me as a visitor, to each of the others, to wives, to world peace, to friendship, to children, and finally to grand-children. I mentioned a new grand-child, Isabella, and our host offered a final toast to her. [*Later, Isabella's mother was ecstatic when I told her that the child had been so honored, and so far away!*] Each toast meant another slug of vodka, so we were a happy crew when we left. Nevertheless, our travel schedule was severely disrupted. We still had a long way to go.

We stopped next at a point of land overlooking the city of Goris, the last city in Armenia. It is, for Armenia, a large city, close to Azerbaijan. We met more Security men on the overlook and they escorted us to the border. The road from here on was under construction, unpaved, rutted, pot-holed and, because of recent rains, muddy. We experienced delays for road work, and at one point we waited while giant earthmovers carved out a road for us.

When Karabakh was part of Azerbaijan, the main highway ran to the capital, Baku. The new highway will make travel between Armenia and Karabakh far easier. The "Armenian Highway" has been well publicized, all of my fellow passengers knew about it, and many Armenians have donated money for its construction. It will be completed one of these years, but now it's tough going. The trip would have been far worse were it not for our skillful, and apparently indefatigable, driver. Even when finished, the road will not be one that acrophobic travelers will enjoy. Much of the route runs across high mountainsides. It occasionally drops down via series of switchbacks into villages below, but then quickly finds it way back up to the heights where it snakes across steep slopes that fall away precipitously into deep valleys below.

We saw evidence of recent fighting during a rest stop in Lachin, a village in the occupied territory, formerly part of Azerbaijan. Here, bright red poppies bloom beside the drab and rusted carcasses of military vehicles that lay below the highway. Lachin's walls and buildings are pockmarked with bullet holes and many of the village's buildings are gutted. Its inhabitants are returning only now, two years after the cease fire, to their homes.

Karabakh is green, mountainous and beautiful. Forests cover the peaks; lower down there are miles of lush grassy slopes. The mountains are substantial, and explain why the country is known as "Nagorno" Karabakh. "Nagorno" is variously translated as "high," "mountainous," or "on the mountains." Armine, whose mother is an English teacher, was our grammarian. She said it should be Nagorni Karabakh. No matter, Armenians drop the modifier anyhow, and refer to the newly independent nationlet only as "Karabakh," or by an alternate name, "Artsakh."

At a check point and rest stop, I wrote in my note book: "We have now been on the road for more than twelve hours. Finally, we're approaching our destination, Stepanakert, the capital of Nagorno Karabakh." Just before we arrived we saw a rocky crest in the distance. Our driver tells us that the village of Shushi (or Shusha), the former capitol of Karabakh, was situated right on the crest above steep cliffs. From there, he says it is only a short way downhill to Stepanakert.

We arrived at Stepanakert at dusk. Several physicians and officials were waiting for us at the government hospital. Two were surgeons, older men in worn white lab coats. As Gagik went to talk with them, a white Volga and a Niva arrived and men from the Karabakh security service jumped out, and greeted our KGB man, the other Gagik, with bear-hugs and kisses. The security mens' reunion was more successful than Gagik's encounter with the hospital staff. Voices were raised and there was an angry interchange. Gagik returned shaking his head and muttering something about going back to Yerevan. Clearly there was a breakdown in communication. No arrangements had been made for patients to come to the hospital for us to see, the purpose of our visit. Gagik will meet again with the medical staff in the morning and see what can be worked out.

The Hotel Karabakh, the best that Stepanakert has to offer, is smack in the center of the city, immediately adjacent to the Presidential Mansion. It has seen hard times, but, despite broken fixtures and intermittent running water, our accomodations were adequate. I would have preferred to settle in, but the local KGB had planned a banquet and it was waiting for us at a restaurant some distance from the city. A meal, more vodka, more toasts, and speeches by the mayor and by other local officials. None of us sparkled; understandably, after a long day.

Breakfast the next morning (Sunday) was a pickup meal of lavash and cheese supplemented with granola bars that I brought. Afterwards, Gagik met with the hospital staff. The Karabakh doctors wanted us to stay for the week, to see patients and operate. We had planned only to spend the weekend seeing patients. To stay longer was out of the question; patients were waiting for surgery in Yerevan. As the discussion wore on, I saw that Gagik was becoming increasingly irked. As nearly as I could tell, he blamed the Karabakh doctors for not being ready for our visit. I never did learn—not that it makes much difference—at what level the plan fell apart. Our doctors? The AGBU office in Yerevan? The Armenian Ministry of Health? The Karabakh Ministry? Or with the doctors in the hospital in Stepanakert? Plainly, the chain was too long. I said nothing, but thought that just one phone call would have prevented this confusion. Would our long trip be for nothing? Gagik met again with the doctors. The final decision was that Stepanakert radio would announce that we were here and we would stay long enough to see as many patients as showed up on the following morning.

We spent the rest of Sunday sight-seeing. The Chief of Karabakh Security, Mr. Alexander Aghasarian, accompanied always by several subordinates, was our guide. He is clearly a most competent and efficient person, as might be expected, given the importance of his position. He also seems to be a gracious man. He loves Karabakh and spoke several times of "we and our mountains . . ." He did much to make our stay in Stepanakert pleasant. We drove out of the city to go to Shushi, stopping on our way at an overlook. Stepanakert lay below us, and we could see Shushi on the heights above. Mr. Aghasarian pointed out the progress of the battle for the town. I stepped off the road to see better. Don't stray, he said. The area has not been cleared of mines. I didn't stray. The view was all pastoral; open fields, and flocks of goats grazing on green slopes. They'll help to clear the mines, I thought. Better goats than people.

We drove on to the outskirts of Shushi where we visited the Ghazanchetsots church, said to be the largest of all Armenian churches. Armine laughed when I asked who St. Ghazanchetsots was. No such saint, she said. Ghazanchian was the name of the man who donated the church. It was badly battered during the fighting. The interior was gutted and the white stone exterior lacked the distinctive polygonal dome that distinguishes Armenian churches. Reconstruction was underway, however, and scaffolding showed where the new dome will be.

Shushi was an Azeri community. It occupies a perfect tactical position. I guessed out loud that dislodging the Azeris must have been difficult. Armine translated what I had said and Mr. Aghasarian agreed. Three columns of soldiers fought their way upward, following ridges leading to the summit. From his description, and from the number of damaged buildings, it was clear that Shushi was not taken easily. In the translation that I received, the Azeris were always referred to as "Turks."

A large open meadow studded with rocky outcroppings covers the crest of the mountain. The Azeri troops were here, he said, showering Stepanakert, plainly visible below, with artillery fire. In the other direction, the cliffs that we saw on our approach fall vertically into the valley. The Security men said that the land here was cleared of mines. It was safe to cross and look out over the precipice. The meadow was carpeted with many wildflowers. I identified thyme, buttercups, larkspur, a purple penstamen-like plant, vetch, yellow composites, poppies, a mallow, and wild roses. But this was quite different from other mountain meadows that I have hiked through. Here, a profusion of brass cartridge cases lay everywhere among the flowers.

After seeing Shushi, including another church and a mosque, we drove back down to Stepanakert and then east, well beyond the city, past a town on the road to Baku where where we saw barracks with the red crescent moon and star of the Azeri flag painted on their walls. These, our guide said, were built to house settlers imported from Azerbaijan. The Turks, I noted, had done the same thing after invading northern Cyprus.

We turned off the main road and crossed rich farmland to a swimming hole where several families were picnicking and fishing. The fish were small, but large enough to delight the children who caught them. A picnic was waiting for us on a long table. We were joined by several more KGB men. There were plates of tomatoes, cucumbers, barbecued pork, cheese, bread and lavash interspersed with stands of bottles: soft drinks, cognac, and vodka. After the requisite toasts, the security men huddled at the end of the table deep in conversation, and the rest of us were free to explore the surrounding countryside. Gagik Stamboltsian wanted to swim. A Security man displayed a beefy leg with two wrap-around bandages. He went swimming here and was bitten twice by snakes. Gagik went swimming anyhow. Karen Danielian and I walked around the pond following roads in the fields. Sugar beets grow on one side, and tall grain on the other. Wild-flowers are everywhere.

Security men were our constant companions and their white Volgas and Nivas escorted us on our return to Karabakh. Because the chief was riding with us, police officers at every checkpoint stood at attention and saluted. I wondered aloud why we deserved such solicitous attention. Armine whispered to me that Gagik Melikian is the officer in Yerevan who disburses KGB funds!

On our way we stopped at a massive monument made of square-cut, orange stone. It depicts a bearded man and a masked woman. The woman's mask illustrates a curious Karabakh custom; a bride may not speak to her father-in-law for five years (how did such a custom come to be?). The monument is important to the Armenians of Karabakh, and it is depicted endlessly on buildings, labels, and signs.

The next morning, Monday, I showered. No hot water, only very cold, very bracing, mountain water. The others slept late, so Karen and I walked around Stepanakert. A few buildings were burned out; others showed signs of damage and repair, but I saw no evidence of generalized destruction. We returned to the hotel, and then went to the KGB head-quarters for breakfast. Omelet, greens, potatoes, honey, cold cuts, toast, preserves, and the thickest, richest, most delicious cream I've ever had. [*At home, when I told Barbara about the breakfast, she said that what the Armenians had translated as "sour cream" was most likely "clotted cream," clotted by cooking and known in England as "Devon cream."*] The meal was not only excellent., but instructive as well, for I learned that it is not good for Americans, this American, anyhow, to overeat and drink vodka at breakfast. It makes for a logy morning.

Patients and their families milled around, waiting for us at the hospital. We saw several children with severe burn scars, and a child with a cleft lip. Most of the patients, however, had war-related injuries from gunshot, shrapnel and landmines. As we examined them, I saw how random and democratic bullets and shrapnel are. They strike anywhere. Their flight is unaffected by age, occupation—soldiers and civilians were both represented—or by sex. As the wounded crowded in to be seen, I was reminded that wars don't end when the fighting ends. Not for the injured, and not for war-impoverished countries.

We saw so many patients that I began to wonder if everyone in Karabakh had been wounded. Empty eye sockets, scarred and deformed faces, head wounds and associated traumatic epilepsy, amputated extremities especially of the lower extremity from land mines, the scourge of modern warfare. One encouraging observation is that their fiber-glass prostheses, made by German-trained prosthetists, were superb. I have never seen better.

For many of the patients, there was little that we could offer. Despite their problems, an optimist would have to say that many were fortunate to be alive for they would have been dead if the projectile had struck a fraction of an inch in another direction. Many were candidates for reconstructive surgery. We made arrangements for them to come to Yerevan. Others had retained, but asymptomatic, foreign bodies—bullets, and shrapnel—that did not have to be removed. We reassured these and others, whom we could not help. We told them that their conditions will improve, knowing that "to improve" means that they will, in time, learn to live with the sequelae of their wounds. After the last patient left, we joined Karabakh's Minister of Health and the hospital staff for a final banquet. Food and more toasts of vodka, and a cognac that is made locally. So, despite the initial friction, we parted as friends and started the long trek home.

It was now late in the day. We had hoped to visit Tatev, a monastery perched high on a precipice in Zangezour. After we reached relatively good roads in Armenia we made a run for it and got as far as an overlook perched over one of the most majestic gorges I have ever seen, a spot that equals our natural parks in its grandeur. We could see, in the dusk, the Vorotan River far below us, and the Tatev church in the distance, above a high waterfall. It was now almost dark, and we had to head back. The local KGB men were preparing a cookout, but it was too late and we stopped to tell them that, regretfully, we couldn't wait.

We drove through the night, a trip marked by a long search for petrol and piercing cold as we crossed the summit at the Zangezour border. We arrived in Yerevan in the morning hours, exhausted. The trip was arduous, but now I understood why the Armenians of Nagorno Karabakh fought so hard to keep their mountainous enclave.

The rest of my stay in Yerevan was anticlimactic. The doctors seemed to lack enthusiasm. There was an ennui, a feeling of ho-humness, as if their positions were more or less a sinecure. I felt that the Unit and its mission were no longer a challenge for them. Lack of organization was obvious and disturbing. No arrangements, for example, had been made to see the many patients that we had operated on previously, even though

I had specifically requested this in advance. No provisions were made for us (Cathy Vlastou arrived during the second week of my stay) to operate on patients with special problems, so we ended up caring for whomever showed up. Although we did twenty-six operations, the Armenian surgeons could have provided equally good care for the patients that we operated on.

During our flight back to Athens, we compared our feelings and impressions about Armenia, and about Yerevan. What we saw is like what occurs after a volcanic eruption: Krakatoa, or Mt. St. Helens for example. There is a gradual reestablishment of flora and fauna as a new ecosystem becomes established, a phenomenon now well underway in Armenia. Our impressions included such minutia as the never-ending sound of scores of dogs barking all night long, now worse than before. Of the bright neon lights in downtown Yerevan, mostly on "poker parlors." Of girls in shorts! A fair number, too, never seen on past visits. Of how terrible the roads still are. Of how much new construction there is; of new houses, many lavish and ostentatious, and of other buildings as well. Of how traffic fills the streets—downtown Yerevan now has a five o:clock rush hour! There have always been a few expensive cars, but now there are many more BMWs and Mercedes. Of the new restaurants and cafes like the classy Holsten bar whose balcony overlooks Mashdots street, the city's most pleasant thoroughfare. Attractive waitresses serve excellent Holsten beer and good snacks. Unlike two years ago, however, amenities do not come cheap. Prices are now commensurate with that of similar establishments throughout the world. Of how people on the streets are better dressed, and actually seem happier Of how many more stores, more goods, more street markets we saw. Of how there's no more caviar to be found at any price. The Caspian, lacking any regulation by its bordering nations, has been polluted and fished out. Of how much the service at the airport has improved. Arrival and departure have been streamlined. It's still no Kennedy, but at least it's tolerable.

Our feelings about the AGBU's Yerevan Plastic and Reconstructive Surgical Center are more complex. We know that we'll not return—too many things bothered us on this visit. Lack of organization and apparent lack of interest, most notably. Lack of effective leadership, always there under the surface, is even more apparent. More attention should have been paid at the very beginning to recruiting the personnel who would go to the states for training. Some were good choices, others not so good. Long distance recruitment without direct contact and interviews was not the best way to go. For the future, if the AGBU plans to continue to support the Unit, it should allot funds to train young surgeons, Leon and Karen for starters. They both show promise. Where there are well trained surgeons, there will be quality surgery.

Appendix A

The Early History of the Armenian Church and Its Martyrs

The Armenian church came into being because two men, the Armenian ruler Tiridates the Great, and the Christian missionary St. Gregory the Illuminator, met during the closing years of the third century A.D.

The Persians overran Armenia, an ally of Rome, in the middle of the third century. Diocletian had become emperor of Rome in 284 A.D. Rather than lead his legions against Persia as his predecessors had done, and in so doing suffer defeat and humiliation, Diocletian wisely took another course. He gave military support to Prince Trdat, the son of the Armenian king whose assassination had led to Armenia's downfall. Trdat had been brought to Rome as a child, to escape the marauding Persians. There, as Diocletian's protégé, he received his education and military training. In time he became known as a physically strong, fearless soldier and leader.

Diocletian supported the Armenian prince with the understanding that he would attempt to wrest Armenia away from Persia. First, Trdat used diplomacy to gain the support of Armenian nobility, and then used his army to drive out the Persians and expand Armenia's borders. As ruler of Armenia, Trdat became known by his Romanized name: Tiridates, later Tiridates the Great.

Meanwhile, in Rome, Diocletian, alarmed by the growth of Christianity, aggressively worked to stamp out the religion. Christianity had spread to Armenia and elsewhere. Tiridates, following the Roman emperor's lead, martyred many Armenian Christians including St. Gayane, St. Hripsemeh, and their companions. The story of the Armenian martyrs began, according to legend, in a nunnery in Rome; Gayane was the Superior of a Christian religious order and Hripsemeh a beautiful young follower. Diocletian saw a painting of Hripsemeh and ordered her to be brought to him. The women fled, however, first to Alexandria and eventually to Armenia. Diocletian, sent to Tiridates, asking him to kill Gayane and return Hripsemeh to Rome.

Tiridates sent for the maiden. She refused to come to him. He was infuriated. In one version of the story. Hripsemeh was stoned to death, in another she was roasted and torn limb from limb. Gayane, and thirty five other Christians were also massacred (October 5th is the Christian martyrs' day on the Armenian Church's calendar of saints). A week later Tiridates became seriously ill.

The legend of Saints Hripsemeh, Gayane and their companions may be myth, nevertheless it appeared early in Armenian church history. At the least, it seems safe to assume that a band of Christians were massacred. [N.Y., Butler, Alban *Lives of the Saints,* vol. 3, Herbert J. Thurston, and Donald Attwater, Eds., 1955]

Armenian history now takes a strange turn. Sometime during the last half of the third century, a Christian missionary, Gregory, came to Vagharshap (present day Echmiadzin) from Cappadocia. According to early Armenian writings, Gregory had been a boyhood acquaintance of Trdat, and had also fled Armenia as a child to escape Persia's armies. Unlike Trdat, however, he was brought up as a Christian. The accounts also suggest that, by a great coincidence, Gregory's father had assassinated the Armenian king (Trdat's father), an event that led to the Persian conquest of Armenia.

Gregory was ordained a priest in Cappadocia. He may also have been named Catholicos of Armenia, even before his arrival there. His dates (ca. 240-330) suggest that he was middle aged or older when he arrived in Armenia, old enough to hold a position of responsibility. He had gone there, presumably hoping to convert Trdat. The king would have none of it, however. He tortured and then imprisoned Gregory in a dungeon at the Khor Virap monastery, on Armenia's western border where he was fed and kept alive by a wealthy woman, and where he remained, underground, for twelve years during which time Trdat continued to persecute his Christian subjects.

Trdat's illness, following closely after the massacre of Saints Gayane and Hripseme and their companions, was widely believed to be God's punishment. His illness may have been mental, for lycanthropy (the belief that one is a wild animal) was one of his delusions (in another version he was turned into a boar). The king's sister learned in a dream that Gregory would be able to cure her brother. She begged Trdat to release him. He did so. Gregory treated him, and the king recovered. Grateful for his miraculous deliverance and impressed with the power of Christianity, Trdat, his court, his family, and the people of Armenia became instant Christians. Thus, Armenia became the world's first Christian state in 301. Gregory was known thereafter as St. Gregory, the Illuminator.

It was a time of miracles. The Armenian church teaches that, after the king's conversion, Gregory "saw a vision in which Christ with a radiant face descended from heaven and marked with a golden hammer the place where the first Armenian church was to be constructed." (The name Echmiadzin means "The Sacred Altar of the Saviour's Descent.") A cathedral, completed in 303A.D., was built on the spot.

Much of the above is clearly apocryphal. The coming of Christianity to Armenia was not the bolt from the blue that church tradition suggests. Christianity spread centrifugally outward from Nazareth, interpreted and taught by Paul of Tarsus and by other traveling apostles. St. Eusebius, historian of the early church, suggests that the Apostles Matthew and Bartholemew may have taught Christianity in Persia and Armenia. Matthew is believed to have died naturally in the Persian city of Hieropolis (Mabog) on the Euphrates river, while Bartholemew is said to have been flayed and beheaded on the shores of the Caspian sea, in what was then part of Armenia. Christians were active in Armenia for more than a century before Gregory appeared on the scene. Evidence for this may be found in several early sources and in Eusebius's writings. These even suggest the presence of bishops in Armenia, particularly in Siunik, prior to Gregory's arrival.

It is difficult to know how much of the original cathedral at Echmiadzin remains. It was extensively rebuilt at the end of the fifth century by Vahan Mamikonian, a prince of Armenia, and further restored on several occasions since. Whether or not one believes in Gregory's vision, it must be admitted that the chosen location was convenient, for, in keeping with early Christian practice, the present church was built on the site of a pre-existing pagan church.

The Armenian Apostolic Church is one of the five oriental Orthodox churches (Armenian, Ethiopian, Coptic, Syriac, and Indian-Malabar) all of which are autocephalous. Its creed is based on the Bible and on the doctrinal resolutions of the first three Ecumenical Councils: Nicaea, (325); Constantinople (381) and Ephesus (431). It repudiates, however, the resolutions of the Council of Chalcedon (451) which tried to end a divisive argument about Christ's nature, an argument that was then tearing Christianity apart. The last council concluded that Christ had two natures, human and divine. The Armenian church, however, in company with the other four Oriental Orthodox Christian churches, did not accept the compromise and split away from the Eastern (Greek) Orthodox church. Unlike the western churches, the Oriental Orthodox churches remained monophysite (from the Greek *mono*, one and *physis*, nature). They believe, and teach, that Christ's divine and human natures are united in one body, rather than divided. The Armenian church differs in another way, to its eternal credit it does not—unlike most Western Christian churches and subsects—subscribe to proselytism.

Appendix B

The Armenian Genocide

The massacres and deportation of the Armenian people are among the twentieth century's most brutal events. The events leading up to and surrounding what is now known as the Armenian genocide are as follows.

In the last years of the nineteenth century, revolutionary groups became increasingly active in Russia. Their fervor spread to Armenia where two organizations came into being. Both had strong elements of nationalism, but one, the *Dashnaks* ("Revolutionaries"), wished to introduce socialism, with a distant goal of an independent Armenia. The second organization split from the more moderate Dashnaks in 1887 to become the *Hnchaks* ("*hnchak*" means "Bell" the name of their newspaper), the more militant of the two groups. The Hnchaks' immediate goal was to liberate Turkish and Persian Armenians and form a unified Armenian state. Armenians living under the Turks were passive and lived with their oppression. The impetus for freedom came not from the Armenian population, but from the militant Hnchaks who organized demonstrations in Istanbul to protest oppression.

Ironically, Russia knew how Turkey would respond to Armenian revolutionary activity, and attempted, unsuccessfully, to put down both the Dashnak and Hnchak factions in Armenia. In 1890, the Hnchaks demonstrated in Istanbul. Amil Hamid II, the "Bloody Sultan," responded as Turks always responded and the infamous Hamidian massacres followed during which the Turks slaughtered thousands of Armenians. The Hnchak's revolutionary fervor and its bloody aftermath alienated their supporters and the group faded away. Soon, however, the Dashnaks took up the cloak of militancy and their provocation led, in 1895 and 1896, to further slaughter. Kurdish forces sanctioned by Hamid killed between one and two thousand Armenians in Istanbul during those two years.

Terrible as this slaughter was, it was only a preview to the genocide that followed in 1915 and 1916, during the early years of World War I, in which an estimated one and a half million Armenians, mostly in eastern Turkey, were killed or forcibly displaced. (As with all such events, numbers vary. Available evidence, based on reliable contemporary accounts, range between one and two million deaths).The Turk's excuse was that the Armenians were disloyal to Turkey and were aiding the enemy, Russia. And a genocide—though the word was coined later—it was. The Armenian population in Anatolia, according to one estimate, was reduced from about two million to less than 25,000.

The Turks have denied in the past, and they continue to deny, that the 1915 and 1916 atrocities occurred, just as certain groups today deny that the Jewish holocaust occurred. The evidence for both happenings is, of course, overwhelming and totally convincing.

Appendix C

The 1988 Armenian Earthquake

The 1988 earthquake involved much of northern Armenia. The casualties were highest in Gyoumri, the country's second largest city. Tragically, the earthquake struck at nineteen minutes before noon on December 7, 1988, at a time when the city's buildings were full. The initial tremor lasted for a minute. It was was followed four minutes later by a stronger after-shock measuring 6.9 on the Richter scale. Many thousands died instantly, as houses, apartments, schools, factories, hospitals, public buildings—in fact, every building in Gyoumri more than two stories high—collapsed in a great cloud of dust. Thousands more simply disappeared and survive today only as casualty figures.

The quake's epicenter was twenty-five miles north of Gyoumri and several smaller communities closer to the epicenter were virtually annihilated. The town of Spitak was destroyed and almost all of its inhabitants died. The cities of Stepanavan and Kirovakan also suffered enormous damage and casualties. The first estimate was that 10,000 had died in the quake. The estimates continued to climb over the following weeks, to 45,000 and eventually to 60,000. Finally, there was no way to obtain an accurate count; some believed that as many as 100,000 may have died (one final estimate was 55,000.) Although most of those who were caught in the collapsing buildings died instantly, many thousands more suffered injuries. The scene immediately after the earthquake was a preview of hell. An estimated 400,000 dazed and homeless souls wandered about, amid smoke, fire, death and desolation.

The quake's effects spread far beyond the area of the actual damage. It was a difficult time both for Armenia and for the Soviet Republic. Only ten months earlier, Armenia and Azerbaijan had gone to war over Nagorno Karabakh. During the ensuing months, 100,000 Armenian refugees had come to Armenia from Azerbaijan; many of these displaced persons were in the earthquake zone and became disaster victims. Their unregistered presence is one of the reasons that an accurate count of the casualties was so difficult to achieve.

The Soviet government immediately transferred thousands of soldiers to aid in disaster relief. Many came from Azerbaijan where they were trying to quell the ethnic strife that was driving Armenians out of the country. When the Soviet soldiers left Baku, Azeri mobs attacked Armenians and burned their homes. The transfer of soldiers to Armenia resulted in still another tragedy. A plane carrying seventy-nine Soviet soldiers from Karabakh crashed while landing in Leninakan (Gyoumri) on the Sunday following the quake; all died.

Soviet President Mikhail Gorbachev was in New York City meeting with President Reagan when the quake struck on Wednesday. On learning of the extent of devastation, he cut short his stay and returned to Moscow, arriving there on Friday and in Leninakan the following day. It was important that he go, for it was a chance to gain support for *perestroika* (lit. "rebuilding"), his program of political and economic reforms.

Armenians were disdainful of Gorbachev, and they continue to speak badly of him. First, he refused to help when this intensely nationalistic state pushed for independence. Later, his refusal to referee the Nagorno Karabakh problem served to precipitate war between Armenians and Azerbaijanis. Gorbachev needed to do some fence-mending. The earthquake was an opportunity to build support for himself and confidence in the Soviet government.

Meanwhile, organizations in the US, Europe, Latin America and elsewhere offered to send relief. The Kremlin requested America's help for the first time since the end of the second World War. Within days, military planes loaded with medical equipment, doctors, and trained rescue personnel arrived, first from neighboring Soviet states and then from European countries and the United States. Relief agencies in the United States, and particularly the AGBU, were quick to raise funds. Americans, many of Armenian descent, pledged millions of dollars. Their donations eventually helped to found the Yerevan Plastic and Reconstructive Surgical Center.

One may ask why the toll of this earthquake was so high compared to other recent quakes of the same magnitude. The answer lies in Soviet construction practices. Knowledgeable seismologists, architects, and builders had warned about the disgraceful inadequacy and shoddiness of construction in this earthquake-prone area. Buildings were too high. Many were built of unreinforced, thick concrete slabs held together only with mortar. Corruption also contributed to building flaws. To save money, builders added illegal amounts of sand to the concrete that went into buildings.

The woeful inadequacy of Soviet construction practices is evident when the 1988 Armenian earthquake is compared with other quakes. The Mexico City earthquake of 1985, which struck a much more densely populated urban area, was far stronger, measuring 8.1 on the Richter scale, yet fewer than ten thousand people died. The 1989 earthquake that struck San Francisco, a city built to withstand earthquake damage, measured 7.1, yet only 63 people died. Finally, the earthquake that shook Los Angeles on 17 January, 1994, measured the same as the one that devastated Armenia; fewer than 40 deaths occurred in Los Angeles.

What about product liability? Who were responsible for the faulty design and the shoddy construction that resulted in the deaths of so many thousands of Armenians? While undoubtedly many individuals were culpable, ultimately it is the Soviet system that must bear the blame. The Soviet government promised that Gyoumri would be rebuilt after the earthquake. One hundred and fifty thousand construction workers flooded into northern Armenia with a goal of rebuilding two million square meters of housing over the next two years. A year later only one apartment complex was completed (*Pravda*, quoted in *Scholastic Update*, Dec.15, 1989). Then, with the Soviet breakup, all construction came to an end and the city remained as I saw it in 1993.

Appendix D

Armenia in the Twentieth Century

During the first World War, Turkey chose to ally herself with Germany, a decision which immediately precipitated war with Russia. By 1917, Russia had occupied much of eastern Turkey, including the cities of Kars, Erzerum, and Trebizon on the Black Sea, and the lands around Lake Van. This territory (Anatolia) had been Armenian, but now its cities and countryside were empty, for the Armenian population had been decimated or driven out by the Turks during the 1915-16 genocide. Armenia needed that land. There were many refugees in Little Armenia waiting to return to their homes. It was an option that would have been open to them, had it not been for the unfortunate advent of the Russian Revolution.

Russia was soon being consumed by the Revolution's internal strife. Russian troops were withdrawn from Turkey to return to Russia where they were used to quell internal disorder. Ethnic Armenian troops who had been fighting on other fronts were recalled to replace the departing Russians. The Russian departure allowed Turkey to reorganize. Armenia, Georgia, and Azerbaijan, threatened by a bellicose Turkey, formed a Federation of Transcaucasian States. It was an alliance that was doomed from the start. Fighting broke out among its ethnic groups (the seeds of the Karabakh conflict were planted at this time). In the end, the Muslims dropped out to form Azerbaijan and the Georgians formed Georgia, leaving Armenia to stand alone.

Even before the 1915 genocide, Western nations were struggling with "the Armenian question." At the end World War I, Woodrow Wilson decided that the US would protect those Armenians who had survived Turkish massacres and deportation. The American Senate, however, led by Republican Henry Cabot Lodge of Massachusetts, would not accept this commitment. So Armenia, unloved and unwanted except by its own people, had no recourse except to make peace with the Turks and become an independent, stand-alone state. This, the first Armenian republic, came into being in July 1918.

Conditions within the new republic were grim. Yerevan was filled with starving, disease-ridden refugees. Some help came from the west, but not enough to prevent an estimated 200,000 more deaths from starvation. During this time, a militant Turkey managed not only to revive her army, but on another front was preparing to drive the Greeks out of Asia Minor.

The new Republic of Armenia struggled on against nearly impossible odds. Still, the dominant political party, the Dashnaks, made progress in forming a new government. Urged on by the British, the Armenians now marched into eastern Anatolia to take back the lands occupied by the Turks. It was an unfortunate miscalculation, based on Armenia's belief that they would be supported by Britain, by other European nations and by the US. No support was forthcoming and Turkey fought back. Again the Turks prevailed; they marched into Alexandropol (later Leninakan, now Gyoumri) in November of 1920. Again, Armenia had no choice but to make peace with her nemesis. At this point, and with little resistance from the Dashnaks, Armenian communists rose to take over the government and immediately asked to become a part of the new Soviet Union. In 1922, Armenia ceased to be an independent entity. The country was occupied by the Bolsheviks and became part of the Soviet Union, a step which served to preserve the Armenian state as an entity and that led seventy years later, with the USSR's dissolution, to the formation, in September of 1991, of today's Republic of Armenia.

Bibliography

Alexander, Edward
A Crime of Vengeance: An Armenian Struggle for Justice
NY, The Free Press, 1991

Arlen, Michael J.
Passage to Ararat
NY, Farrar, Straus, Giroux, 1975

Azarian, Levon
Armenian Khatchkars
Yerevan, Editions Erebouni, 1978

Burnaby, Capt. Frederick
A Journey On Horseback through Asia Minor
Oxford, Oxford University Press, 1996 from 1898 edition

Bitov, Andrei (trans. By Susan Brownsberger)
A Captive of the Caucasus
NY, Farrar Straus Giroux, 1992

Bryce, Viscount
The Treatment of Armenians in the Ottoman Empire 1915-1916 Documents presented to Viscount Grey of Fallodon
London, His Majesty's Stationery Office, 1916

Chahin, M.
The Kingdom of Armenia
NY, Dorset Press, 1987, 4th printing

Diuk, Nadia and Adrian Karatnycky
New Nations Rising: The Fall of the Soviets and the Challenge of Independence
NY, John Wiley & Sons, Inc.,1993

Farson, Negley
The Lost World of the Caucasus
NY, Doubleday & Company, Inc., 1958 (also published as *Caucasian Journey*, London, Penguin, 1988.)

Holy See of Echmiadzin
Armenian Churches
Lisbon, The Calouse Gulbenkian Foundation, 1970

Hovannisian, Richard G.
The Armenian Genocide: History, Politics, Ethics
NY, St. Martin's Press, 1992

Mandelstam, Osip
The Noise of Time and Other Prose Pieces
London, Quartet Books, 1988 reprinted from 1965 edition

Marsden, Philip
The Crossing Place: A Journey among the Armenians
Harper Collins Publishers, London, 1993
Kodansha International, N.Y., 1995 (American Edition)

Rost, Yuri
Armenian Tragedy: An Eye-Witness Account of Human Conflict
NY, St. Martin's Press, 1990

Sandwith, Humphrey, M.D.
A Narrative of the Siege of Kars
London, John Murray, 1856

Selby, Bettina
Beyond Ararat: A Journey Through Eastern Turkey
London, Abacus, 1993 2nd reprint

Simpson, C.
*The Spendid Blond Beast: Money, Law, and Genocide in the
Twentieth Century*
NY, Grove Press, 1993

Suny, Ronald Grigor
Looking Toward Ararat: Armenia in Modern History
Bloomington and Indianapolis, Indiana University Press, 1993

Walker, Christopher J.
Armenia: The Survival of a Nation
London, Routledge, 1980 (revised edition with new material, 1990)

—

Architectural Monuments In the Soviet Republic of Armenia
Leningrad, Aurora Art Publishers, 1971

—

The Armenian Earthquake Disaster
Madison, The Sphinx Press, 1989

—

Yerevan: A Guide
Moscow, Progress Publishers, 1982